LOW COST HIGH PRICE

'This book will touch your heart, inspire your mind and challenge your soul. It will make you weep at the futility of lost lives, help you to understand the work to save women caught up in the sex trade and give an insight into the amazing people who found the core skill to make a difference – unconditional love.

'In my work with children and young people, listening to them on the telephones in ChildLine or seeing them in court as teenagers, it has always been clear that their experiences of abuse led them into the darkness because of their own lack of self-esteem. In this remarkable story you will discover that it is possible to restore their humanity and so enhance our own.'

Baroness Howarth of Breckland, OBE

'This book gives an excellent insight into the lives of those damaged by prostitution and the hope, love and opportunities that are offered by those who respond to offer help and support. Theresa's story is one of inspiration and hope.'

Mark Wakeling, Director, Beyond the Streets

'*Low Cost High Price* is a powerful testimony to God's Hope and Healing. Theresa Cumbers's own life story of triumph over loss and despair through trust in Christ is the backdrop for her surprising call to ministry with women in prostitution. I rejoiced as I read the stories of transformed lives, because of the unconditional love of Christ as shown to the women through Theresa and her colleagues. This book can serve as a "primer" for all those who seek to follow Jesus' directive to serve "the least of these". It describes a project which has not only responded to the winds of God's Spirit, but also is sensitive to the standards of good practice and government policy. Be prepared to be inspired and educated about how God's light is shining into the darkest of corners of this world!'

Revd Dr Lauran Bethell, International Consultant, Women's and Children's Issues, International Ministries, ABC-USA

'*Low Cost High Price* is a must-read book for two reasons.

'Firstly, it is the story of an ordinary Christian who is challenged by God to do something extraordinary. From sitting on a J.P.'s bench and, as it were, holding judgement over young prostitutes, she feels challenged to go out and meet these young girls and love and care for them and demonstrate real Christian love. Her story will challenge all of us that we can make a difference and God can use us.

'Secondly, this book shows us something sad about our own society, that on the streets of many, many cities of England are young girls forced to sell their bodies. These girls are there largely because they are forced to be there by drug dependency or unscrupulous people. This is not the glamorous end of prostitution as shown by recent television programmes. This is not people making a choice because they want more money. This is, sadly, hell on earth; these young women have run out of options. This book shows what can be done by Christian groups and others and how these women can be given dignity and help and a way out, so there can be for them life beyond the streets.

'I highly recommend this book.'

Laurence Singlehurst, Director, Cell UK

'Theresa Cumbers has captured well the challenge and Christ-centred character of her work among women who are frequently held of little account in our society. She writes tenderly, yet without illusions. She speaks of graces given, some victories won and a few tragic disap-pointments. She traces a journey of understanding and compassion, as well as the building of a ministry exer-cised imaginatively in the name of Jesus Christ.

'Jesus was accused of keeping bad company. It's one of the reasons why the gospels are so compelling. Who would ever invent a religion where the central figure mixed with the disreputable? Jesus also recast the mould of those who were favoured by God. He said the poor in spirit would inherit the Kingdom of Heaven. The poor in spirit are people who know their need. Theresa writes about the humanity and humility of many of the women (and the occasional man) with whom she's worked over the years. Many of them know their need. Most have no pretence. That's what makes this book so truthful, real and encouraging.

'It's been a joy to have been associated in a small way with Theresa's ministry over the past decade. I'm glad that she found in Martin Down someone able to help her record a remarkable story with a continuing challenge for us all.'

The Rt Revd Graham James, Lord Bishop of Norwich

'Theresa's story is a powerful and moving account of the efforts of herself and many others in the Magdalene Group to improve the conditions of life for very many women in Norwich who turned to prostitution. Her story shows how the commitment of every individual can change our society for the better and I thoroughly commend it.'

Charles Clarke, former Home Secretary and MP for Norwich South

LOW COST
HIGH PRICE

Hope for Women Trapped in Prostitution

The Story of the Magdalene Group

Theresa Cumbers

with Martin Down

Authentic

First published 2010 by Authentic Media
Milton Keynes
www.authenticmedia.co.uk

British Library Cataloguing-in-Publication Data

A catalogue record for this book is available from the British Library

ISBN 978-1-86024-798-9

Cover design by Rachel Myatt
Printed in Great Britain by Cox and Wyman, Reading

This book is dedicated to the women of the streets –
May God grant you your heart's desires.

ACKNOWLEDGEMENTS

I want to express my thanks to my two children, Estelle and Benjamin. As young people they supported me all the way as I stepped out in obedience to God to reach the women of the streets. There were times when they, as much as I, had to trust God that he would care and provide for us all. He did.

I also want to thank Martin Down, who was also God's provision for me in getting this book written and published.

CONTENTS

FOREWORD

by Maria Landon

author of *Daddy's Little Earner* and *Escaping Daddy*

Theresa Cumbers is a formidable and charismatic woman who opens our eyes and ears to the realities of life on the streets. Without any doubt, this is an extremely important book for our time and we can no longer ignore the issues it raises. Thankfully, books are now being written and read that reveal a world that society has in the past chosen to ignore.

Theresa shows us a world of darkness, misery and despair, but interlocked throughout these pages is a love that fears no obstacles – a love that transcends all the desperation, filth and degradation that accompany a life of prostitution. Theresa shows us that we all have a role in these desperate people's lives, and that role is, quite simply, to love each other as Jesus loved us. Even without the Christian ethos, I believe we all have a responsibility to help one another and support and care for each other. You do not have to be a Christian to learn something from this book – its issues are extremely relevant to all of us. We can no longer ignore these issues: children, women and men are literally dying out there on our streets because they think nobody cares. If they are not murdered by their abusers, pimps or punters, they will likely be killed by (often enforced) drug or alcohol addictions. Even if they survive, their lives are dogged by mental health problems, abusive relationships and feelings of hopelessness and despair. We have to show them another way, show them that they do have a choice, show them that it is never too late, and they and we must never give up.

Theresa is a remarkable woman who radiates an unconditional love for everyone she meets but especially the most vulnerable people in our society. Her story is an exquisite example and a remarkable testimony to what love can achieve and shows us that even through our own personal tragedies we are all able to do something to help those out there with so much need.

INTRODUCTION

This is the story of the Magdalene Group, a Christian outreach to women working as prostitutes on the streets of Norwich, England. By the grace of God I was one of those who launched this work in 1992, and over the years, as its director, I have seen it prosper and grow. My engagement with these women changed me as much as I hope it changed some of them. So this is also my story, the story of how God took me from poverty in the East End of London to a successful business career in Norwich, and then to finding a new sense of fulfilment in sharing the lives of these damaged people on the streets of the city.

I have wanted to write this book for two reasons. Firstly, in order to change people's attitudes to prostitution, by showing what life is really like for those on the streets. For most people (including myself before I became involved in the lives of these 'working' women) prostitution is a murky world of dark streets and furtive assignments. It is a world in which the women, and sometimes the men, who are selling their bodies are regarded with a mixture of disgust, prurience and incomprehension. There is a small group of people claiming to represent so-called 'sex-workers', who maintain that this is a legitimate lifestyle that some women choose, and in which they should be recognized and protected. But judging from my own experience, I would say that there are very few women who engage in 'the world's oldest profession' who do so voluntarily. Of all the women I have met on the streets, I would say that not one of them had entered or remained in prostitution as a free choice.

So why are they there? And what keeps them there? I have tried to write a book that shows the reality of the lives of people trapped in prostitution. It is a way of life that is very far from glamorous or exciting. Indeed for the most part it is a way of life that is sordid, dangerous, and degrading to all the parties involved, whether they are the ones buying or the ones selling the sexual encounters. Although there are men involved in prostitution as 'rent boys', the majority of prostitutes are women, and the lives of these women are usually chaotic. Their problems have mounted up one on top of another: drugs, alcoholism, homelessness, debt, ill health, children taken into care, broken family relationships and abuse, until the woman has virtually lost control of her life and is locked into a pit of despair from which there does not seem to be any way out.

But secondly, I have wanted to write a book that shows that there are ways out. These women and men are human beings like the rest of us. They have committed sins and experienced failures, they have made mistakes in life – but then so have we all. Jesus came to seek and to save the lost, and amongst the lost he specifically included women of the streets. So we set out in the Magdalene Group to meet the women on our own streets, and to find out how we could meet their needs.

The psychologist Abraham Maslow identified a hierarchy of human needs, starting with the most basic physical needs for food and shelter, and leading up to the more spiritual, inner needs for self-esteem and hope. We had to start at the point at which we met each person and to meet those needs in any way that we could. We discovered that more than anything else these women needed love; more than anything else it was that of which they had been deprived. With love and much practical help, through the co-operation of many different agencies, we found that these women and men could be enabled to break free of their past and begin a new life.

I have told the stories of many such women in this book and of a few such men. Some are 'success' stories, where the women have come away from a life on the streets and found love, home, family, work and self-respect. Some have found faith in God and in his Son, Jesus. Other stories do not have such happy endings: they are the stories of people who knew that they needed help but were somehow unable to reach out and receive it; of people who tried but failed to make the break with the past. Some stories I have been able to tell at length because we knew these women over a long period of time and saw them change. Others are mere fragments of a person's story: a woman who made contact with us at the Magdalene Group, took a step or two towards her goals and then disappeared back into the night from which she came. That is the reality of such work. Sometimes it is frustrating, sometimes desperately sad, but at other times infinitely rewarding.

The Magdalene Group was only one of a number of such ministries that God was raising up, both in England and around the world, during the 1990s, and we found ourselves building relationships with other similar groups to the enrichment and benefit of us all. Our work also brought us into contact with many secular agencies both statutory and voluntary. It was important for us to

be recognized by these other agencies as credible partners in helping the women we were contacting. To that
end we had to establish and maintain the highest standards of compliance with all the rules and regulations
governing work with vulnerable adults and children
and, more than that, to gain a reputation for excellence in
our own field. So successful were we in this that the
Magdalene Group was eventually invited to be involved
in the Government Review of the law concerning prostitution. There is an ongoing debate both in this country
and throughout the world about how prostitution
should be treated by the law. This debate has the poten-
tial to change the lives of those engaged in prostitution
and to influence public attitudes to the practice of paying
money for sex. So we saw it as part of our service to the
women we met, to engage with this debate at the highest level. But the focus of our work was always the individual, the unique story and the unique needs of each
one.

◆ ◆ ◆

Of the stories I have told here, that in Chapter 1 is the
story of Gemma Adams, one of the women murdered in
Ipswich in 2006. It is a tragic story. I did not know
Gemma personally – the story I have told is drawn from
press reports at the time of her murder and details that
emerged subsequently during the trial of her murderer,
Steven Wright.

In telling the stories of other women whom I have
known personally, I have in most cases used pseudo-
nyms to preserve their anonymity. One or two of the
women have seen what I have written and agreed to
their real names being used. Some of these women now
speak openly about their past and encourage and help

others to take the road out, as they have done. These are brave people who have confronted their demons and walked a difficult path – the way out is rarely quick or easy. Their past, like the past of ex-prisoners, is rarely a recommendation in terms of finding employment or accommodation. But their stories will help us all to understand more clearly the nature of the problems that they have faced, and perhaps be moved to do something ourselves to bring hope to others still caught in the trap of prostitution.

1

TWO STORIES

Gemma kissed her boyfriend goodbye and walked off down Handford Road. They had lived together for several years in a steady relationship, of sorts. But Gemma was off to earn money by selling herself on the streets of Ipswich. It was already ten o'clock at night when they parted and the streets were quiet. To some, it might seem a strange sort of relationship in which a man walks away from his girl-friend late at night leaving her to be molested by strange and perhaps dangerous men. But in the world in which Gemma now lived this was not an uncommon arrange-ment. Jon did try to keep in touch with her while she was out, by texting or phoning her on her mobile phone, but there was little he could do if she was in trouble.

It was mid-November and Gemma was warmly dressed in her black, zip-up jacket and blue jeans, her handbag over her shoulder. Apart from her mobile phone, her handbag only contained a toothbrush and toothpaste and a clean pair of knickers – all necessary after the acts she would probably be asked to perform that night. It was no pleasure servicing the sexual desires of lustful and sometimes violent men, but the craving for another hit of heroin or crack cocaine was so strong that she was driven to go on doing it.

She waited in one of her usual spots, standing back from the kerb in the shadows. She recognized one or two of the other girls further down the street. One of them, Tania, had been missing for about two weeks, but girls came and girls went, and who knew where Tania had gone? It was a Tuesday evening. Not the best for trade, in her experience, but within a few minutes a car came cruising slowly along the road. She did not know this particular vehicle but took a step forward to show herself to the driver. Sure enough, he pulled up and wound down the passenger-side window. A short conversation followed and Gemma got into the car and drove away with the man. She asked for the money before they started. She liked to have the money safely in her bag before she performed whatever acts they asked her to. There were men who, if you were not careful, would push you out of the car afterwards without paying. But then, on the other hand, there were girls who would take the money and run before the services had been performed. There was no point in anyone appealing to the police; the encounter was illegal in any case. It was just a jungle. They drove to an unlit car park that she often used with her customers. Afterwards, he drove her back to the red-light district and dropped her off to wait for another punter.

Gemma was a pretty girl: long hair, naturally blonde, high forehead, blue eyes. She spoke well, and some of her clients would say, 'What's a nice girl like you doing out on the streets?' She had started to take drugs when she was still at school – nothing serious, just a bit of cannabis at parties. Then she went on to Suffolk College to study for an NVQ (National Vocational Qualification) in Health and Social Care. It was there that she met her boyfriend, Jon, and there that she was introduced to harder drugs. At first she could control her habit, and after college she got a job with an insurance company. It was not what she had planned for herself, nor what her parents had wanted her to do but it provided the money that she needed to live and to buy drugs. But soon her drug habit was interfering with her work. She would come into the office late, or not at all, and when she did come in she was sometimes unfit to carry out her tasks. In the end she was fired, but the craving was insatiable. Without a job and a pay packet at the end of the week, Gemma had only two options – theft or prostitution. She took to prostitution.

She had scarcely contacted her parents for two years. They had been aware of her growing dependence on drugs and had tried to help her. At their insistence, she had seen a doctor and started a course of methadone treatment. But she was soon back on heroin and unable to face her parents. She had not even been home for Christmas for the last two years, and although she realized how much this hurt her family she could not hurt them even more by showing them the sort of person that she had become. Her parents still tried to contact her on her mobile phone from time to time, and sometimes she texted them back to say that she was well, but even this tenuous conversation had lapsed recently. Her family now had no idea of the life she was living.

The family home was in a village on the outskirts of Ipswich, a comfortable middle-class community of commuters and business people where Gemma had grown up. It was in many ways an ideal childhood: Brownies, piano lessons, ponies, a dog called Holly who had been rescued after being abandoned in a shed. There were no clues at this stage to the course that Gemma's life was to take, except that drugs are an ever-present menace in Britain today, and anyone's daughter or son can fall into the trap.

Now Gemma was 25 years old and there was no one to rescue her from herself and her addiction. She had worked for a few months in a massage parlour (often a polite, twenty-first-century name for a brothel). At least the work was safe and the surroundings comfortable, but the management took a large slice of her earnings and they were no more sympathetic than the insurance company to the effects of her drug habit. Some of the customers at the massage parlour began requesting Gemma by name, and she began to give them her own telephone number. She could then arrange for them to come and visit her at her own flat – that way her earnings were all her own. So she left the massage parlour and went freelance, but the visits from her regulars were not enough on their own and she had to resort to the streets.

That Tuesday night actually proved to be a busy one. By 1.15 in the morning she had already had three clients and was back on her beat wondering if there would be any more. She had earned £75 that night, enough to supply her needs for the next twenty-four hours, but more would be useful. A dark blue Ford Mondeo crawled along beside the kerb and Gemma stepped forward again into the light . . .

At 2.55 a.m. Ipswich police received a phone call from Gemma's boyfriend Jon. He was worried about his girl-friend: she had not answered her mobile phone for an hour and a half. At first the police were not inclined to take the problem seriously, until Jon explained that Gemma had been working on the streets. At this point alarm bells started to ring. Tania Nicol, another prosti-tute, had been reported missing a fortnight before. Appeals for her to come forward and make contact with her mother or the police had gone unanswered and people were beginning to wonder if her disappearance might be suspicious. Now here was another woman reported missing from the same area.

Had Gemma gone home to her family? It seemed unlikely, given her recent lack of contact with them, but the police had to check this possibility before instituting any further enquiries. The moment when Brian and Gail Adams were confronted by a policeman on their doorstep telling them that their daughter was missing is one that they will never forget. The policeman told them that their daughter had been working as a prostitute on the streets of Ipswich, and they were concerned to establish her whereabouts, in view of the earlier disappearance of Tania Nicol. At that moment, the nightmare of Gemma's loss to the family only became worse. The idea that their daughter had become a prostitute shocked and shamed them. How had their popular, pretty little girl sunk to this? How had they let this happen to her? Could they have done more to help her with her addiction? Could they have done more to keep in touch? There is very little that loving parents can do when hard drugs are involved, but they were racked with guilt and sorrow, even before they knew what had happened to their child. They lived every day in a state of suspense as, still, no news of Gemma was heard.

Seventeen days later, the water bailiff at the Hintlesham Fisheries, just a couple of miles outside the town, was walking the Belstead Brook. It had been raining for several days and he wanted to see if any debris had been washed down and blocked any of the watercourses on his beat. The brook was in full spate and, not far from the road, where a bridge crossed the stream, there did seem to be something blocking the river. There was a bend where a tangle of twigs and leaves were caught on something wedged in the angle of the river. The bailiff waded into the stream and started to pull the debris away. He saw two white humps sticking up out of the water. It looked like the behind of a shop-window mannequin. But as he moved more of the tangle of debris he saw that it was the bottom of a real woman, naked except for a pair of earrings.

Not stopping to investigate any further, he telephoned the police and told them that he thought that he had found a body in the water. Before long the area was cordoned off and forensic teams were examining the body as it was removed from the brook.

It was Gemma Adams.

Her body, already naked, had been thrown into the fast-moving water from the bridge, to be carried downstream until it met with some obstruction. There were no signs of violence on the corpse and, because of its immersion in water, no clues on it as to how it came to be in the water or who had put it there.

Gemma's was the first of five bodies to be found in the countryside around Ipswich in the next few weeks. The second to be found, a mile further downstream in the same river, was that of her friend Tania Nicol. All five had been working as prostitutes in the town, all were naked and all had been strangled. The serial killings made headline news across the country and abroad. The resources of the Suffolk Police were overwhelmed by the complexity of the investigations and the intensity of the manhunt that followed. Police from other forces across England were drafted in to help.

The murder of a prostitute is not uncommon. On average, there are ten prostitutes murdered each year in England and they rarely command more than a few lines in the local paper. It is as if the life of one of these women is of little worth in the eyes of society. It was only the serial nature of these killings in Ipswich that caused a national sensation.

Eventually a man called Steven Wright, who lived in the same area of Ipswich in which the women had worked, was arrested and charged with five counts of murder. The trial took place at Ipswich Crown Court a year later and Wright was convicted, and sentenced to life imprisonment. But nothing would ever bring back Gemma Adams.

◆ ◆ ◆

Forty miles away, in Norwich, Cara had also been working as a prostitute. Cara was even younger than Gemma when this had all begun – still in the first bloom of her youth. Cara had been introduced to prostitution by another woman, Jo, for whom she had started to babysit. Jo was working as a prostitute on the streets of Norwich and she needed a babysitter to look after her daughter while she was out at night. At the age of 17 Cara had already developed a drug habit and needed increasing amounts of money to pay for her drugs.

Cara had suffered much sexual abuse as a child. Up to the age of 5 she'd had a normal childhood, growing up at home with a mother, a father and an older brother. But from that age onward a friend of her father, a frequent visitor to the house, would take her up to her bedroom and feel her private parts. The abuse never went further than this and Cara, while she felt uncomfortable about it, accepted it and kept 'their little secret'. When Cara was 7, her mother started to work during the day at a local pub. She would take Cara with her and leave her with Jack, the landlord, while she did her work. In the private sitting room at the back of the public house, Jack would sit with Cara watching pornographic videos. He also began to abuse her and eventually penetrated her. Each time he did so, he gave her sweets and a £5 note in return for keeping 'their little secret'. Having 'little secrets' with men seemed to this young child to be a normal part of life.

In her early teens several other men took advantage of Cara's vulnerability and abused her, culminating in a final betrayal of trust within the family. Cara had always been especially close to her grandmother and had been able to talk to her about things that were important to her, although she had never confessed to anyone the sexual abuse that she was suffering. But when Cara was 11 her grandmother had died. Some years later, when Cara was visiting her widowed grandfather, he raped her. He told her that he was determined to be the one to enjoy her virginity. Little did he know.

When she was 16, Cara's parents divorced. Her father had been having affairs with a number of other women, and he finally left the family home. Cara applied for a place of her own and was allotted a flat in the centre of Norwich. In her new apartment she soon met the neighbour, Jo, who had a young daughter called Lucy. Cara had been smoking cannabis since she was 14, but now Jo introduced her to amphetamines. Jo began to ask Cara to babysit for her while she went out shopping, and soon the babysitting became a regular evening appointment while Jo went out onto the streets. One evening Jo asked Cara if she would like to earn some money for herself and do her a favour at the same time. Jo had started a period, but had three punters booked to visit her that night. She gave Cara some phone numbers and Cara made arrangements for these three men to come to her own flat instead. Thus Cara moved almost imperceptibly from being the victim of serial sexual abuse in the family, to being the victim of serial sexual abuse in prostitution.

Cara had been working as a prostitute for about two years when she, together with Jo and Lucy, came to see us at the Magdalene Group. The Magdalene Group had been set up some years before to offer help to the women of the streets, and at the time I was the director of this organization. Cara developed the habit of calling in to see me at the drop-in centre that the Magdalene Group had established in the red-light area of the city. We would share a cup of coffee and a chat. I told her that our door was always open and that we would be willing to help her in any way that we could. Over a period of time Cara came to trust me and confide in me.

Cara was frightened of going out onto the streets. She was aware of the dangers for women in her situation, and she was also frightened that she might meet some-one in the city who knew her. Her mother was unaware of the direction in which her daughter's life had gone. Cara confided in me that she hated the things that she did. She had a dream of one day meeting a man who would love her for herself and not for money, and who would marry her and give her a little house and children of her own.

One day Cara came to the drop-in in a terrible state. She tried hard not to engage in penetrative sex with her clients. Many of them were content with oral sex or fan-tasies of bondage and sado-masochism. But the previous night she had once again had full penetrative sex with a customer. Afterwards she had felt so dirty and unclean that she had bathed in strong bleach and had continued to wash and scrub herself until her skin and her private parts were burnt and raw. Cara was frightened to go to the hospital for treatment; she was suffering from depression and ill health quite apart from this latest self-inflicted injury. But Toni, our pastoral worker, persuaded her that they should go together. The doctors and nurses treated her and prescribed for her and referred her to her own doctor for continued care. During her consultation

the doctors also discovered that Cara had a pelvic disease that would prevent her from ever having children of
her own. She knew that she had already had a number of
miscarriages, but this news was a bitter blow.

One night, when I was working late in the office of the
Magdalene Group, I received a phone call from Cara. It
was wintertime and a storm was raging outside. She was
in great distress and talked of committing suicide. She
felt that she could not carry on. She had nothing left to
live for: the constant craving for drugs, the endless
search for the money to buy them, and the disgusting
things that she found herself doing night after night,
were too much for her to bear any longer. As I listened to
her sobbing over the phone I was praying and asking
God what I should do. I was seriously concerned that
Cara would indeed take her own life if I could not come
up with something or someone to help her. I had often
been tempted to take the women and girls that we met
into my own home, but I had always realized that I
would be taking on burdens that I could not bear myself,
and burdens that I could not inflict on my own children,
grown up as they were.

I had been in contact for some months with a
Christian woman called Jan who lived out in one of the
market towns in the countryside and who had a special
gift for helping young people with drug addiction. She
was not part of any organization, whether statutory or
charitable, but she would take young addicts into her
home and help them. I had occasionally visited her
house and been impressed by the work that she was
doing there. I told Cara that I would find somewhere
safe for her to go that very night and I would pick her up
from where she was in 15 minutes. It was already 11 p.m.
I phoned Jan who said, 'Bring her over straight away
and I'll find somewhere for her, even if only for the

night.' So Cara and I drove out into the country in my little Mini, through the wind and rain to an address that Jan had given me. Neither of us will ever forget that night: the Norfolk lanes seemed so narrow and winding in the dark, the gale buffeting the car and the windscreen wipers struggling to keep up with the downpour. The address turned out to be that of a local pastor who, with his wife, was prepared to take Cara in and look after her while Jan fixed up something more permanent in her own house.

This was the beginning of a new life for Cara. She stayed with Jan for more than a year, during which time she came off the drugs and even began to mentor some of the other young addicts, boys and girls, who lived in the house. Jan held a weekly prayer meeting, at which she invited Christians whom she knew in the town to come in and share their stories with the boys and girls living in the house. This often led to the boys and girls wanting to know more about Jesus for themselves, and one evening it was Cara who asked Jan to pray with her for Jesus to come into her life and help her to start afresh with him. She started to go to church and later she was baptized; the church continued to give her unconditional love and support. I would go out and visit Cara from time to time, and although there were often problems in the house I could see her blossoming as a person and growing in her faith. But there was no quick fix for her traumas and confusion. She continued to suffer a sense of intense loneliness and found it difficult to believe in her own worth.

Eventually Cara moved back to Norwich. The church in which she had become a Christian continued to stand by her and support her, but when she moved back to the city she missed this community of friends around her. I was still in touch with her and she still came to the drop-in to talk to me. I could see her drifting back into her old lifestyle, which she did for a time, but she now had more resources of her own to pull herself out of it. Throughout this period, in spite of the backsliding, Cara was maturing in character and gaining self-respect. She knew what she wanted now, and even in the face of her setbacks she fought hard to preserve her dignity and her values. At the age of 21 Cara wrote a long letter to both her mother and her father, telling them about all the abuse that she had suffered since childhood and about her life since leaving home. Her mother was horrified and confessed in turn that her own father, who had raped Cara when she was 15, had also abused her. This was the beginning of a new relationship between mother and daughter.

In 2001 Cara met a young man with whom she fell in love. To him, also, she confessed everything and bravely he took her as she was. They faced many difficulties in the early days of their life together with financial, personal and health problems, but they persevered together and their relationship grew stronger through it. Cara knew that she needed once again to make a fresh start and to move away from the city and her old contacts. A baby was on the way! They were both so excited when they found out that she was pregnant, and they wanted to bring up their child in a safe environment. They found a small house in a country town and made it into a lovely home. Although she had been told at the hospital that she could never bear children, miraculously, Cara carried the baby safely, and once her daughter was born both of Cara's estranged parents became regular visitors to the family, and relationships were renewed that had once seemed broken forever.

A good number of years have passed since I first met Cara. She is now 32 years old. She has survived. I have kept in touch with her and, although she is still troubled by negative feelings about herself and her past, she still has faith that with the help of God she can work through them. I am pleased to say that Cara now has a future and a hope. She has a man who loves her and cares for her – for herself and not for money – and whom she loves. She has a daughter of her own and she has her own home in the Norfolk countryside. Her dreams have come true.

◆ ◆ ◆

Two stories: one with a tragic ending, the other with a happy ending. Two young people trapped in a life of drugs and prostitution. What was it that made the difference to the outcome for them? Part of the difference, at least, lay in the fact that Cara found help in her time of need: people whom she learned to trust, in whom she confided, who loved her and believed in her, even in the days when she did not love or believe in herself. It has been our privilege over the years at the Magdalene Group to be able to offer that sort of love and help to many women like Cara.

But the Magdalene Group was not always there in Norwich, and I was not always involved in helping girls like Cara. Once upon a time I had played a very different role in their lives.

2

ON THE BENCH

'Let's see what excitements we've got in store today!'

We were assembled in the magistrates' room drinking coffee, and the chairman of the bench was examining our list of cases for the day which he had just been handed by the clerk. I had been appointed as a Justice of the Peace about three years before this, and I sat on the bench two or three days a month.

'Spot of bother, I see, on Saturday night outside the Red Lion. Again! That licence really needs to be reviewed; that place is nothing but trouble. Three twits in the same street without a television licence. Coming to your neighbourhood soon – the little green detector van. One soliciting. One drink-driving. And – oh no! Our friend Ethel has been relieving Marks & Spencer of their stock again.'

The chairman was a senior magistrate, who knew not only the trouble spots in the city but many of the troublemakers as well.

'But we don't know this hooker, do we? Is she new on the block? Louise Valerie Ashton? Haven't seen her before. In any case, drink up. It's nearly ten. Time to kick off.' And he led the way into court.

'All stand,' announced the clerk, and everyone dutifully stood as we filed in and took our seats on the bench.

It was sometime later in the morning that Louise Valerie Ashton was called. The usher led into the dock a pretty girl, 18 years old, tall, well dressed in high heels and a tight skirt, her fair hair neatly pinned up in a French pleat. But she was obviously terrified.

The clerk asked her to confirm her name: 'Are you Louise Valerie Ashton?'

We waited for what seemed to be a long time for her answer. The girl was gripping the rail of the dock and looking down in despair. There was the faintest sound of trickling water: she had wet herself. There was a painful silence. A grim female usher began to approach the dock.

'Should we adjourn?' the chairman asked the court in general.

'No,' the usher replied harshly, 'get it over with. We'll clear up later.'

'Continue then,' the chairman said to the clerk. So the clerk read out the charge.

'Louise Valerie Ashton, you are charged that on the night of 16 May this year you were loitering in King Street in this city with intent to solicit for the purposes of prostitution. How do you wish to plead? Are you guilty or not guilty?'

'Guilty,' came the whispered reply.

The prosecuting solicitor briefly outlined, for the benefit of the magistrates, the circumstances of the woman's arrest, adding that there were no aggravating factors: she had been seen by a police officer loitering in the street and then talking to a man through the window of his car. The chairman looked around. Was there anyone to speak for her? A solicitor, a probation officer, a friend? Were there any mitigating circumstances? But the girl seemed to be without any supporters at all.

Who was this girl? I was wondering. What was she doing on the streets? We had heard a rumour that some of the university students were trying their luck at prostitution to supplement their grants. Was she one of those? Where was her mother or her friends? Could no one have come to court with her to give her some moral support? Was she too ashamed of what she had done to tell anyone in the family or her friends? And who was going to take care of her after this brief hearing, help her with her wet knickers and tights, take her for a cup of coffee and comfort her. I thought of my own daughter Estelle, nearly the same age as this Louise. I wanted to mother her, but here I was sitting in judgement on her.

Of course I believed in law and order and the administration of justice. Without it we could all be murdered in our beds. It was against the law of England to keep a brothel, to live off immoral earnings, or to solicit as a common prostitute. If that was what this girl had been doing then the law required that she should be fined. If she persistently failed to pay her fine, the court would have to send her to prison. But was that really what this girl in front of us needed – a fine or imprisonment?

We, the three magistrates on the bench, held a quick consultation and agreed on the minimum fine for a first offence. 'You may go now.'

Louise Valerie Ashton left the court quietly sobbing in shame, either for having prostituted herself or for having wet herself, or both. I never saw her again. But she was the last straw for me. I knew for certain now that I was on the wrong side of the bench. My place was alongside women like Louise, helping them not punishing them. The time had come for my life to take yet another new turn.

◆ ◆ ◆

I had come from a very poor family in the East End of London, born at the beginning of the Second World War.

One of my earliest memories was of being bombed out of our house. We were only a few miles from London docks and so we suffered many air raids during the Blitz. I was the youngest of seven children, five older brothers and one older sister. Our father was away in the army. One night, my mother roused us as the sirens wailed and took us all out to the air raid shelter in the back yard. She covered me with a blanket and put my teddy over my face. We could hear the bombers droning overhead and then the bombs began to fall. The crumps and explosions were getting nearer and nearer, and then a bomb landed right on our house. The roof of the air raid shelter came down and I was buried in the debris.

The others managed to clear a way out. Mercifully no one was seriously hurt. At first my brothers thought I was dead. But they pulled the teddy off my face and there I was alive, if shocked. My mother was taken with us to a neighbour's house where she was offered a cigarette. She had never smoked in her life before, but that night her hair turned grey and she became a smoker.

We were rehoused in another terraced house a few streets away. This one, like our first house, had just two bedrooms and a tiny box room. Throughout my childhood my parents had one room, my five brothers shared the other, and my sister and I squeezed into the box room together. We had no electricity and no indoor toilet. The house was lit by gas-lamps, with their fragile white mantles. The toilet was out in the yard. There was no bath or bathroom. When I was small my mother bathed me in the copper in which she did the washing, but later I was allowed the first turn in the tin bath in front of the fire.

Looking back over more than sixty years, I am so proud of my parents: they worked so hard to support us and look after us all. After he came out of the army, Dad returned to his work as a bricklayer, and Mum earned money wherever she could. She cleaned for some rich people in Ilford; she picked strawberries and dug potatoes in the fields beyond Barkingside; she even had a barrow outside the railway station. In addition to which, of course, she cooked and cleaned and ironed and mended for us seven kids and Dad.

But people should not think that poverty necessarily meant squalor. I suppose some people might have said that we lived in a slum, because of the lack of 'mod cons'. But Dad kept the back yard immaculate. He kept chickens in a little coop, and every year he painted the old air raid shelter, the chicken-coop, the fence and anything else he could see, white. He planted our tiny patch of earth with flowers, especially stocks and roses, and whenever I smell their scent I am reminded of Dad. And we were not a miserable family. Whatever we lacked in the way of money or possessions, we made up for in love.

Nor should people think that poverty meant selfishness – quite the contrary. There was a real community spirit in those East End streets, especially during and after the War. We never had much for ourselves, but I can remember Mum lending a cup of sugar or tea to friends or neighbours, or giving away potatoes or other vegetables that she had gleaned off the land.

The playground for us children was the bombed out gasworks behind our house. It was a sea of rubble, water-filled craters and old tunnels infested with rats, with a solitary chimney from the coke ovens still standing. In order to belong to the gang, each child had to climb up the iron rungs inside this chimney and appear out of the top. No worries about 'health and safety' in those days! I was so small that I had to take a handful of stones up the chimney in my knickers' pocket. When I reached the top I had to throw them over the rim of the chimney because I was too small to be seen. But I was accepted into the gang. I was more of a tomboy than my sister Patsy, who was always my dad's favourite little girl.

On Sunday afternoons all my siblings would go out to play and Mum and Dad would settle down for a nap. But I would wait in our front room until I heard the Salvation Army band strike up at the end of the street. They stood in a circle in the road (we did not have many cars in those days) and played the old hymns and salvation songs. As soon as I heard them, I would run out to join them. There was a stout lady who was the Major. She would always welcome me with a big hug, and say, 'Here's our Theresa,' and give me her tambourine to play. I would accompany the band as they moved round our streets and we ended up at the little mission hut, where we were all given a hot drink and a biscuit.

No one else in our family ever had anything to do with church, but I learnt the old hymns and songs, like 'What a friend we have in Jesus' and 'Jesus loves me, this I know, for the Bible tells me so'. I did not have a Bible to tell me so, but somehow I learnt that Jesus loved me from those dear, old-time Salvationists. I certainly prayed in those days. A few years later, we seemed to have a lot of funerals in our family. Dad was never keen to go, but Mum would say, 'Don't worry, you don't have to come. My Theresa will come with me because she prays and knows the Lord.' I also remember that when I was waiting for the Army to come on those Sunday afternoons I would sit in our front room talking to someone and singing songs – in a strange language.

I did not like school. I think the other children made fun of me for my patched and darned clothes and my brother's hand-me-down boots. So I did not do particularly well at lessons, except for art. After I left school at 15, I went to Pitman's College where I took every course I could: shorthand, typing, bookkeeping and accountancy. My mum thought I was ever so clever, and what I learned there certainly stood me in good stead for the rest of my life.

I got a job with a timber and plastics company in Essex. Some years later, I made friends with a girl called Brenda who worked in the same office. Brenda was depressed because her husband had left her, so I suggested that we should go together to some ballroom dancing classes. I thought it would cheer her up if she met some new people. The classes were called 'Refresher Classes'. For Brenda they might have been refreshers, but for me they were the first time I had ever tried this form of exercise. There were, of course, some men at the dance hall and I was old enough to be interested in them.

I'd had one serious boyfriend before, at the age of 18. We had 'walked out' together and held hands in the cinema. But he was a Jew and I was a Gentile, and so the idea of marriage was not welcome to the families on either side. In the years before the War there had been a good deal of overt anti-Semitism in the East End of London. Sir Oswald Mosley had found it a fertile recruiting ground for his British Union of Fascists. I don't think that my own parents were particularly prejudiced, but such attitudes were difficult to avoid. And of course Jewish families were always against their offspring 'marrying out'. In any case, for whatever reason, the two communities did not intermarry. So my teenage passion came to nothing; but I did love him.

Now at the dancing classes there was a very short, older man who seemed to have taken a fancy to me. Whenever the teacher said, 'Take your partners,' he would literally come running over to ask me to dance. I, however, was not so pleased with him. He barely came up to my shoulder, so that I had to dance looking over his head, while he looked – I don't know where. He was not even a good dancer; he regularly trod on my feet and laddered my stockings. One day I said to Brenda, 'If that chap comes to dance with me again, I am not coming any more.' Just as I said that, a tall, handsome man, whom I had never seen before, walked into the room. He was extremely smart and well groomed. I looked at Brenda and said, 'Now that is the kind of man I want to marry.'

I spent the rest of the evening trying to catch his eye and flirt with him, but he did not seem to respond. It was the last dance before he came over to me and asked me to be his partner. And that was it. John and I fell in love and were married six months later. He was a lovely dancer, and we had such a happy life together.

No wonder he was smart. He worked as a bespoke tailor for Moss Bros of Covent Garden. We started married life in a small flat in East Ham, but within a year John had been promoted to be manager of Moss Bros in Brighton. When we moved, you would have thought that we were emigrating to Australia. My mum and my sister Patsy waved us off as the removal lorry took our furniture, and even I felt scared. Brighton seemed so far away and so 'foreign' to an East End child like me. It may seem strange today, when people take their holidays all over the world and think nothing of air travel to foreign parts, but in those days even Brighton seemed like another country.

We lived in Brighton for seven years. John decided that we should not start a family for a while in order to give us time for ourselves. In view of what was to happen later, I am profoundly grateful that we had those years together. We moved again, to Llantrisant near Cardiff – which really is another country – and there we started our family. First Estelle, our 'Little Star', and then Ben were born. During this time I managed to get a job as an agent for Portmeirion Pottery. I could fit in my visits to customers around my duties at home. So the job suited me perfectly. Sometimes, during the day, I would take Estelle with me to deliver orders in the valleys, and we would be treated to hot drinks and Welsh cakes.

Our next move was to Norfolk. John had been evacuated to Norfolk as a boy during the War, and although he was born a Londoner, he had loved life in the countryside. He now went into partnership with his brother in the motor business. Although he was used to measuring people for smart suits and army uniforms in a clean white shirt and pressed trousers, he was equally at home in a boilersuit, with oily hands taking an engine to pieces. It did not turn out to be a very good time to start a new business: it was in the middle of the recession in the mid-seventies, but we pulled through and managed to buy our own little house in the village of Chedgrave, a few miles outside Norwich. We loved our life there. It was a very child-friendly village, with good schools at which our two children made friends with whom they are still in touch to this day.

Then one evening in January 1983, John came home and had his tea, then announced that he was going over to Costessey to see his mother, who was ill. It was a foul night, with wind and rain, and I said, 'Do you have to go?' But he was determined. The children, now 8 and 11, clamoured to go with him, so after his favourite dessert of pancakes and syrup, they set off. I can still taste the syrup on his lips as he kissed me goodbye.

Less than an hour later a policeman called at the door. 'Mrs Cumbers? I am afraid that your husband has been involved in a road accident.' There was a long pause. 'I am sorry to tell you that he is dead.'

My world stopped. 'What about the children?' I blurted out.

'They are fine. They have been taken by ambulance to the Norfolk and Norwich Hospital, but we don't think they are injured. If you want to fetch your coat, I will take you in the car.'

Still dazed, I grabbed a coat and went with him into the dark and the wind and the rain, and sat beside him in the police car on the journey to the hospital. He told me that my husband had been waiting at a crossroads to turn onto the main road. A motorcyclist had somehow run into the side of the car. John had died instantly; the motorcyclist had died in the ambulance on the way to hospital. The children were apparently unhurt but had been taken to hospital for observation. Estelle, in the back of the car, had had the presence of mind to reach over and turn off the ignition, because she had smelt petrol. She had unbuckled the seat belt of her brother and pulled him out of the car and over the motorbike. She had then left him on the verge, telling him that she would go and fetch help. She had walked back up the road until another passing car had stopped and asked her if she was alright. She explained what had happened and these kind people had called the police and the ambulance and taken her back to the scene of the accident.

When we arrived at the hospital I could not face going to the mortuary to see John that evening, as I knew that if I did I would not be able to give the children the attention that they needed. I went into the casualty department where they had been assessed and were being cared for. I was allowed to take them home with me that night, and as I tucked them into their beds and kissed them, I said that we would talk more about it in the morning. They understood that Daddy had had to stay in hospital overnight, but the next morning, of course, they wanted to go and see him. I gathered them both in my arms and went into the lounge. We sat down on the sofa together, 'Darlings, I have something dreadful to tell you. I am afraid Daddy won't be coming home again. He has died.'

We all cried, but I knew that I had to be strong for them, and in the end Ben said, as small boys will, 'Can I go out and play football now?' Estelle and Benjamin were so brave. I am sure that there were many days after that when we all wept, separately and together. There were days, I know, when I just hung on to the sink and sobbed till I thought the tears would never stop. The children went back to school. When I picked them up the other mums at first looked the other way; I guess they did not know what to say. In the days and weeks that followed I slowly realized how much closer this had brought us as a family, and how much courage and character the children had shown.

The years that followed were a struggle for us all. There was little money to fall back on, and because of a technical flaw, there was no insurance. I always felt that the insurance company was particularly mean over this, but even that was to be put to good use later. The pain of such a loss lasts for a very long time. The initial shock wears off and some sort of daily life goes on. It has to. But the pain inside is there for much longer.

Six months before this tragedy, John and I had been invited by a business colleague to attend a dinner of the Full Gospel Businessmen's Fellowship International (FGBMFI). This is an event at which someone in an after-dinner speech tells the story of how he became a Christian. At the end there is an opportunity for anyone else to decide to become a follower of Jesus, or to receive prayer for healing, or to be filled with the Holy Spirit.

Through the FGBMFI I had met some wonderful people who supported us and prayed for us after John's death.

Later, I asked if I could bring the children to FGBMFI dinners with me, and John Wright, the president, said that I could. Everyone was so friendly and the children loved hearing the stories. It was at these dinners that both Estelle and Ben committed their lives to Jesus. With Estelle the wheel has now come full circle, for she and her husband and her children are staunch members of the Salvation Army corps in the little town where they live in Suffolk. That godly influence in my own young life has now become the same godly influence in the lives of my children and grandchildren.

It was at one of these dinners in 1983 that I also gave my life to the Lord, and picked up the threads of my own Sunday afternoons with the Salvation Army all those years before. It was not that I had ever completely forgotten the Jesus who I knew loved me then. But my life had been filled with so many other things – husband, work, family and home – that I had never developed the habit of churchgoing. But all along I knew that there was something missing in my life. It was only through the FGBMFI that I finally remembered what it was – Jesus.

But God knew when and how to reach me. Listening to the stories that other people told, I came to realize that I needed to make a decision of my own about how I would live my life from now on. If I was to know God as a Father who loved me, and Jesus as a Saviour who died for me, then I had to become a follower of Jesus and be obedient to my heavenly Father. The joy of taking this step was overwhelming, and I was to need all the resources of strength that this new relationship with God gave me over the years to come.

Now a widow with two young children to bring up, I had to put my mind to earning some serious money. I had done various jobs during our married life. During our years in Brighton I had worked for a big American publishing firm. Now it was time to put my experience of business to good use. I was invited to go into partnership with a friend who had, not long before, started a brokerage, specializing in mortgages, insurance and conveyancing. I was even able to use my own bad experience of an insurance company to pass on good advice and watch over the best interests of our clients.

The firm prospered. I became quite well known in business circles in Norwich. I think I had always had an enterprising spirit; it was John who had been the cautious one. I became President of Women's Aglow Fellowship (the female version of the FGBMFI), and undertook official duties with Business and Professional Women, and Women in Enterprise. We moved to a beautiful new house in Tivetshall. It was during this time that I was also asked to become a magistrate.

The little girl with the darned and patched clothes had come a long way from the East End of London. And yet, through these years, I constantly felt that there was something wrong with my values and the way that my life was going. Here I was, more outwardly successful and respected than I had ever been before, and yet I had a nagging sense that this was not what God really wanted for me. Although necessity had meant that I'd had to develop this career in business, I had a growing feeling that God was calling me to do something else.

In 1989, already approaching 50, again at a meeting of the FGBMFI, I finally surrendered to this sense of God's calling and said to him, 'Whatever you want to do with the rest of my life, I give it all to you.' It is a dangerous prayer to pray. God is inclined to take us at our word. In the early nineties recession struck again and our company was faced with the threat of bankruptcy. What was

I to do now? Where was God taking me this time? I did not know what the future held, but I did know that my Lord would guide me, because for the rest of my life my focus would be entirely on him.

◆   ◆   ◆

One of my colleagues on the bench was Doreen. She was the wife of a church leader in the city. On several occasions we had talked about the prostitutes who came up before us in court. Two things concerned us in particular: the numbers of cases seemed to be increasing and the girls involved seemed to be younger and younger.

In my frustration I would say to Doreen, 'What is the use of us fining them? They don't have any money. That is part of their problem. So what can they do but go back onto the streets and ply the only trade they know, to earn the money to pay their fines. It is like some crazy revolving door. We Christians ought to be out there on the streets helping them.' Doreen had actually taken me up into the red-light district of Norwich and shown me an old, disused church called St Peter Parmentergate which, she maintained, would make an ideal base for such a work. I had already started to meet with six other women who were praying with Doreen for something to happen. Could this be God's calling for me?

And so it all came together, just as it all came apart. Bankruptcy would mean resignation from the bench in any case. That would free me to go out on the streets and get alongside these girls upon whom I had been sitting in judgement these past few years. Louise Valerie Ashton was the last straw. How could I go on ignoring God's call to love them and care for them? Little did I know how much God was going to show me about these women and how misunderstood they were.

I had no idea how God was going to provide for us. Our house was part of the collateral against the company's debts and it looked as if we were going to be both homeless and penniless. I still had two children in full-time education – one at university and the other preparing for university. But if God calls, God provides. In 1992 I put all my trust in him and went out on the streets myself.

3

ON THE STREETS

It was a cold November night when a friend and I, muffled up in our overcoats, ventured out onto the streets where we believed that the prostitutes worked. We armed ourselves with Thermos flasks of hot coffee and chocolate and some chocolate bars, in order to have something to hold and something to offer. We had no idea how we would be seen or received by the women. Would we be sworn at and told to leave them alone? Might we even be physically assaulted? Our hearts were thudding as we walked up to the first woman we saw 'loitering with intent'.

We stopped on the corner beside her. 'Hello,' I said. 'We don't know each other, but I'm called Theresa, and we were wondering if we could offer you any support which you do not already have?'

To our amazement she seemed pleased to see us. She told us her name was Annette. She went over to the wall and beckoned to us to join her. We sat together on the low wall and she started to talk. She was scantily dressed and shaking with the cold. We offered her a hot drink and a chocolate bar, and she was so grateful. As she drank she was shivering so violently that she spilled the coffee over her skirt, but it was her whole life story that came tumbling out. She was being sent out onto the streets by a man who was an alcoholic. If she went home without earning any money, he would simply send her out again until she did. She had been married once. She had loved her husband and he her, but he had been taken ill and she had watched him die, leaving her a widow with three children. I identified immediately with her: I too was a widow, left with two children, bereaved of a husband that I had loved so much. It pierced my heart to think that this could have been me. She had subsequently met another man who she had hoped would look after her, but he had turned out to be an alcoholic, and as soon as he had drunk her benefits he would send her out onto the streets in order to feed his drinking habit. He was her pimp. She did not want to be out there; she did not want to do what she did; but she felt that she was a captive to him.

We offered to meet her for a coffee somewhere the following morning, but she refused. Her man would be at home and would want to know where she was going. So we promised to see her again on the streets and to keep in touch. We told her that we would pray for her safety because we were Christians, and to our surprise she asked us to pray for her there and then. So, sitting on the wall, we prayed that God would keep her safe and help her. As we prepared to leave her to carry on her sorry trade, we were even more amazed when she asked us for a hug. She and I put our arms round each other and I gave her all the love I could in those few moments. To my surprise I felt the warmth of her love enveloping me, not the 'love' for which she was paid night after night by equally loveless men, but a genuine love and gratitude that another human being knew and understood and cared about her.

From that moment I knew that I was in the right place and that God was with us in reaching out, like Jesus did, to these women of the streets. We went on, shaken, not by the animosity or rejection of those we had come out to meet, but by this woman's openness and readiness to receive what we had to give. I knew then that there would be no turning back for me: I would never again be a person who saw such a need as this and did nothing about it.

The second girl that we noticed was younger, only about 19, still fresh and pretty, but wearing a skirt so short it was more like a pelmet. We went up and introduced ourselves as before. She was not unfriendly but said quickly, 'I can't stop and talk. My boyfriend will be coming soon.' She also was shivering with cold, so we poured her a drink and, sure enough, as she was drinking it a young man walked up to us with a distinctly hostile expression on his face. His shoulders were hunched and I seriously wondered if we were going to be beaten up.

'What do you want with her?' he asked. We explained ourselves again and offered him a cup of coffee too. At first he refused, saying he only drank whisky or brandy. 'She's got to work,' he said, but after a few more words he did agree to share a hot drink with us. We left afterwards saying that we would come again another night when perhaps she would have more time.

We saw several kerb-crawlers draw up beside girls and wind down the window. The girls would bend down and discuss terms with the men before getting into their cars and driving off. We prayed for each one as we saw these transactions taking place, knowing that each girl was putting herself in a place of danger by going with a strange man to a lonely place where she might be subjected to all sorts of abuse. My friend and I took down the registration numbers of the cars that we saw, in case any of these girls were later reported missing.

In the daytime this was a perfectly pleasant area of the city, with houses and flats, offices, shops and pubs. But here at night there was a real sense of darkness about it, not just physical darkness but a sort of spiritual darkness, like a cloud all round us. It was the same with the women themselves. As I looked into their eyes I saw darkness. It was as if the lights had gone out inside them. They were living with a darkness within; they had been robbed of the light in their lives. Someone seemed to have robbed them of their very souls.

The third woman we met was in her mid-thirties. We told her that we represented a support group that was willing to try to help women on the streets. At first, she was suspicious and reluctant to talk, but we told her that we had not come out to stop her or interfere with her work, but to give her any personal help she needed. She accepted a hot coffee and a chocolate bar and started to tell us her story. Her name was Rachel. She did not come out every night, she said. She had come out tonight in order to earn enough money to pay the electricity bill. Actually, she had been out the night before as well, but that was because she had a son. His class had organized a school trip to France and her boy was the only one who could not afford to go. Her partner had left her some time ago and she had no other means of paying the bills, let alone pay for school trips to France.

My friend and I finished walking the streets of Norwich at about half past midnight that night and went our separate ways home. It may sound absurd, but I felt elated as I drove home. I could not wait to get back that night and pour out my thanks and praise to God for changing my heart and giving me a passion for these hurting women. And I could not wait to get back on the streets again.

◆　◆　◆

Since the business had collapsed and I had resigned from the bench, God had provided for my children and me in wonderful ways. Our house and my car had all been taken as part of the bankruptcy settlement, so first we had to find somewhere to live. I combed through the local paper looking for properties to let. I noticed an advertisement for an old farmhouse. It looked much too big for the three of us and I was sure that the rent would be too high. But Estelle insisted that we should go and look at it. So off we went. It was a large house with an even larger garden, indeed too big for the three of us by any rational measure. But Estelle and I felt drawn to it as we peered through the windows; we could see ourselves going up and down those stairs and sitting by the Aga in that lovely kitchen. So we sat down on the step and prayed that if God wanted us to have this house, then he would make a way.

To our amazement, all the obstacles disappeared one by one. We agreed an acceptable rent with the landlords, who were a firm of builders. For some reason they preferred us to any of the other five applicants who were interested in the tenancy. But they needed a financial reference. I approached the bank manager with some trepidation. He, of course, knew all about our bankruptcy but he said to me, 'Mrs Cumbers, you have banked here for eighteen years and why shouldn't I give you a reference?' As I came out of the bank I felt as if I was being lifted up and carried along by the angels.

Then we needed an income. I applied to become a carer with various agencies, and I began to work in residential homes for the elderly and sometimes caring for people in their own homes. I liked to work the night shifts. Although this was tiring, it freed me during the day to pursue contacts with the women we were meeting and to follow up other matters to do with our project as it developed. Both my children found part-time jobs to earn a bit of money for themselves, and later we were given permission by the landlord to let out some of our spare bedrooms and take in paying guests. Somehow between us we made ends meet. This period of our lives drew Estelle, Ben and me together as never before. My nearly-grown-up children were marvellous; we supported each other emotionally and became close friends, and all along Estelle and Ben knew and encouraged me in the work that I was doing with the women on the streets.

On one occasion near the beginning, when the cupboards were bare, I looked out of the kitchen window of our farmhouse and noticed that the tractors were harvesting vegetables in the fields. Perhaps it was the memory of my mother gleaning in the vegetable fields of Essex during the War to feed us kids – but the thought came into my mind, 'Why don't you go out and glean?' I went out and asked one of the tractor drivers if he minded if I picked up what was left over, and he replied, 'No, my beauty, help yourself. Any time.' When I had gathered enough for a nourishing soup, I went home and sat down by the Aga. I opened my Bible at random and began to read. I do not think that I had ever read the story of Ruth before, but here I found another woman who had lost her husband, gleaning in the fields and going on to find a new, joy-filled life. God was feeding me with much more 'food' than mere vegetables.

◆ ◆ ◆

I was going out on the streets several nights a week with a number of good friends who were willing to come with me and support me in the work. We always went in twos, because there was an element of real danger. Most of the women had pimps or partners behind them who were making them work and living off their earnings, and here we were offering to help these women and giving them a chance to change their lifestyle.

Sometimes, we were joined by Chris. Chris was a lovely young Christian man whom I had first met when he was doing a soup run for the homeless, organized by the Salvation Army. Chris had been converted only a few years before, and God had given him a particular compassion for the homeless and the hurting. Some nights Chris would drive the car for us and watch out for us at a discrete distance, but we relied most of all upon God for our protection. We would pray every evening before we set out, and at the end of every evening we would give back to God the burden of caring for these women, which was too great for us.

One evening we saw a young woman almost hiding in a hedgerow. We stopped and offered her a drink, which she refused, but when we came back later she was still there and this time she accepted our offer and started to talk. She said her name was Josephine. She had been living in Norwich for fourteen years. At that time she was being pimped by a woman who expected her to earn £100 a night. She had frequently been beaten up if she had failed to do so, and several times she'd had to go to the accident and emergency department at the hospital with injuries to her head and neck. She had always told the doctors that she had been in a fight, but had never said any more. She had run away, but her pimp had found her and brought her back to the flat that she rented for her in the city. She said that she lived in fear of her life. She was too frightened to go to the police. We gave her our mobile phone number and told her that if she was ever in danger she should phone us for help. There was to be a sequel to this story, but at the time I was simply appalled by the tale that she told.

Another woman we met was called Rosie. She had her beat in a dark alley, away from the main streets. She was a drug addict and an alcoholic. Sometimes we would find her actually lying on the ground in some sort of stupor. She told us that she would sell herself for as little as four cans of lager. Low cost – high price! There would be more to tell about Rosie also in the years to come, but at this stage we were simply establishing a presence on the streets, making friends with the women and trying to win their confidence.

The more we learned about the lives of these women, the more painful it became. We often felt overwhelmed by the sorrow of their stories. What could anyone do to help them, to begin to unravel the tangled skein of their lives, to comfort them for the hurts that they had suffered and continued to suffer? We soon realized that the first thing that they needed and that we could give them was love – love that was not conditional on them changing their lifestyle or jumping through hoops to please us or to earn our approval, but love for them as they were in all their troubles and misery. But we realized that our love had to be love in action: a cosy hug might be welcome and might be rare in their lives, but these women needed so much more than this. They needed practical help with life's daily problems – with money, with housing, with child care, with ill health, with addictions, with abusive relationships, the list seemed endless. Above all we realized that, at the deepest level, we could not help these women at all. Their need for self-worth and a sense of their own dignity could come only from knowing the God who had created them and loved them and the Saviour who had come to die for them.

◆   ◆   ◆

I realized that if I were to be of any real help to these women, I needed to be better informed about their trade and to make contact with other people engaged in the same sort of outreach, if there were any. I started to comb through the bookshops and libraries for books that shed some light on the lives of these women. I discovered that prostitution exists in several different forms. There are 'call girls' who often work from home and advertise their wares in public phone boxes or magazines. Brothels are illegal in the UK but they still exist, often disguised as 'massage parlours'. Women work as 'escorts' in clubs, especially clubs that offer some form of sexual entertainment such as strip clubs. Women selling sex through such channels as these can be invisible to the outsider. Especially since the enlargement of the European Union in 2000, there has been a serious increase in the trafficking of foreign women to work in these establishments. These women are virtually sex slaves and are particularly difficult to see and to reach. But it was particularly to the women working on the streets of Norwich that God was calling me.

You can go to the streets of any large town or city in the evenings and in the areas where there is nightlife you can see hundreds of young, single women, scantily dressed and obviously available for sex. These girls may be promiscuous, but they are not prostitutes: they give their favours to the men they meet, rather than sell themselves to them. Indeed their own sexual gratification is probably uppermost in their minds rather than any favours they may be doing for their casual partners. Street prostitutes, on the other hand, are not to be found amongst the noisy throng of clubbers and pubbers. They are more likely to be found on the comparatively quiet streets and corners of a residential district, where few members of the public pass, except those looking for their services. Neither the prostitutes nor their clients want to make themselves too obvious.

In such a district a woman will establish a 'beat' – a corner or stretch of the street where she will stand and wait for her customers or 'punters'. There will probably be other prostitutes in sight, but the women are often jealous of their beats, and cat fights can develop if one invades the territory of another. Unless there are complaints from the local residents or businesses, the police tend to tolerate prostitution in such a district; it is easier for them to keep an eye on such activities if they are confined to a certain area, and the proximity of other women offers them all a degree of protection.

Surfing the Internet I discovered one or two other projects in Britain that were engaged in outreach to these women. I made contact with Paul who was the manager of a similar organization in Walsall near Birmingham. I went over to visit him and to learn how they operated. They had recruited and trained a number of volunteers to go out on the streets and befriend the prostitutes, just as I had been doing. I was inspired by Paul's dedication to the work. He was an ex-addict and knew that most of the women were addicts too. I also visited a centre in Dublin, the Catherine McCauley Centre, run by Catholic nuns. They befriended prostitutes working on the waterfront, and they had a similar non-judgemental approach. We all saw these girls more as victims than as offenders.

In those early days, we were also developing contacts with other agencies whose work might overlap with ours. On the one hand we did not want to duplicate or compete with what other people might already be doing, and on the other hand we wanted to learn as much as we could about what other services were available to the women we met. So we had meetings with the police and discussed their policies and procedures in dealing with prostitution. We had meetings with social workers who might be involved over the custody of children. We talked to the drug agencies. We made contact with doctors and health workers. We needed to build up relationships of trust, not only with the women themselves, but also with other people with whom we would have to work if we were to offer the women real help.

I think at the beginning we were viewed by many of these agencies with a certain amount of suspicion. Perhaps my record as a magistrate and a businesswoman in the city gave me a degree of credibility, but I am sure that many people regarded us as grey-haired do-gooders from the twinset-and-pearls brigade. I could not remember many twinsets or pearls in the East End of London where I grew up, but if that is all we were, then we could have found many other people to do good to, without going out on the streets at night, in all weathers, where many women would be fearful to go at all. This was not a fluffy experience for any of us, not for the women already out there, nor for those of us who chose to join them. It taxed our eyes and ears, our bodies and souls, and broke our hearts.

Once a month, I met with the group of women who had been praying about this particular need before I joined them. We now prayed together over every step we took and discussed the things that I was learning. These women would be praying for us as we went out on the streets at night. Toni became a particular prayer partner of mine and Doreen was a wonderful sounding board. It was this group of women who began to explore further with me the possibility of using the redundant church of St Peter Parmentergate as a base for our outreach. This church, like so many of the medieval churches in Norwich, had been out of use for many years and was now held in trust by the City Council and leased to the

Norwich Historic Churches Trust. It was ideally situated for our purposes in the middle of the red-light district.

When we first got permission to look inside, it was not an encouraging prospect. There was no electricity in the building and no running water. The main part of the church had been used for some sort of storage and was just a mess: covered in bird and bat droppings, plaster crumbling off the walls, broken relics of ecclesiastical furniture, everything smelling of damp and decay and running with rats and mice. But there were two smaller rooms, one upstairs and one down that we could adapt for our use and we agreed with the Historic Churches Trust to take out a lease and begin a project of restoration, at least on the two small rooms for our own use.

For this purpose we formed a charitable trust, with a body of trustees who would be legally responsible for every aspect of the work. We called ourselves the Magdalene Group. In the Gospel of Luke chapter 7 there is a beautiful story of an encounter between Jesus and a woman of the streets:

> Now one of the Pharisees invited Jesus to have dinner with him, so he went to the Pharisee's house and reclined at the table. When a woman who had lived a sinful life in that town learned that Jesus was eating at the Pharisee's house, she brought an alabaster jar of perfume, and as she stood behind him at his feet weeping, she began to wet his feet with her tears. Then she wiped them with her hair, kissed them and poured perfume on them.
>
> When the Pharisee who had invited him saw this, he said to himself, 'If this man were a prophet, he would know who is touching him and what kind of woman she is – that she is a sinner.'
>
> Jesus answered him, 'Simon, I have something to tell you.'

'Tell me, teacher,' he said.

'Two men owed money to a certain money-lender. One owed him five hundred denarii, and the other fifty. Neither of them had the money to pay him back, so he cancelled the debts of both. Now which of them will love him more?'

Simon replied, 'I suppose the one who had the bigger debt cancelled.'

'You have judged correctly,' Jesus said. Then he turned towards the woman and said to Simon, 'Do you see this woman? I came into your house. You did not give me any water for my feet, but she wet my feet with her tears and wiped them with her hair. You did not give me a kiss, but this woman, from the time I entered, has not stopped kissing my feet. You did not put oil on my head, but she has poured perfume on my feet. Therefore, I tell you, her many sins have been forgiven – for she loved much. But he who has been forgiven little loves little.'

Then Jesus said to her, 'Your sins are forgiven.'

The other guests began to say among themselves, 'Who is this who even forgives sins?'

Jesus said to the woman, 'Your faith has saved you; go in peace.'

In Christian tradition this woman has always been identified with Mary Magdalene. As the followers of Jesus we wanted to offer the same love and compassion and forgiveness to the women on our streets.

I was appointed by the trustees to be the first manager of the Magdalene Group with oversight of both the development of the street work and the renovation of the building. I had always enjoyed interior design and I had a vision for these rooms as a place of rest and sanctuary for the women working on the streets, a place where they would be safe and warm and welcome. It would also be a place where we could meet the women during the daytime and talk about their practical and spiritual needs. So for two years we raised funds and took the vision forward step by step.

Again we needed to consult with the people whose lives would be affected by our activities. We contacted the residents of King Street in which the church was situated and we explained what we hoped to do there. We encountered little opposition but much support for our vision. In the evenings before the centre opened we would often meet the women off the streets in the church porch, where we would dispense our usual drinks and chocolate bars and chat to them about their needs. We told them about the restoration project in the church and asked them what they wanted in a place of their own. They, in turn, became excited about the vision.

In February 1995 the rooms were ready. Downstairs there was a shower, a toilet, and a small kitchen in which we could make hot drinks and simple meals. Upstairs we made a sitting-room, where the girls could relax, warm their cold feet, talk and feel safe. I furnished the sitting room as beautifully as I would my own. We had cream walls and red settees and armchairs, wooden occasional tables and a sideboard, books, pictures, lamps and ornaments. We wanted to provide these women, so often despised by the world, with the very best. Some of them came, together with our trustees and supporters, to our opening night. During the course of the evening as we shared drinks and canapés, one of the girls off the streets said to me, 'Why are nice women like you bothering with trash like us?'

What could I say?

'You are not trash, my dear. God loves you.'

4

WHY ARE THEY THERE?

Even while I was sitting on the bench I found myself asking, 'What are these women doing on the streets in the first place? They must realize how dangerous their situation is out there. Why do they go on doing it?' It was only when I went out on the streets myself and started to win the confidence of some of these women that I began to discover the answer to these questions, and many of the stories that I heard broke my heart. I was totally unprepared by my own experience to encounter the depths of pain and misery that filled these women's lives.

The whole subject of prostitution is surrounded by fantasies. Both men and women use prostitutes to project onto them their sexual fantasies. The men who buy the services of prostitutes, the punters, often pay the prostitutes to act out their fantasies for them, asking them to do things that their wives will not do. But both men and women fantasize about prostitutes in their imagination. Women fantasize about being prostitutes and the things that they would be required to do. Men and women enter into the fantasies of films like *Pretty Woman* and television programmes like *Secret Diary of a Call Girl*. In such fantasies the 'hooker' or 'call girl' is a woman who chooses to make this her profession and in it finds glamour and excitement. But nothing could be further from the sordid and brutal truth of life on the streets.

One of the girls that we met on the streets that first night, the one that was wearing a skirt so short that it was scarcely more than a pelmet, was a young woman who we got to know as Natasha. We met her again on many occasions and worked hard to help her over a number of years. She was only 19 when we first met her. She was pretty, well dressed and well spoken. She had grown up in a middle-class family that lived in a big house in the country and had ponies and other animals. Her father was a well-to-do businessman and Natasha had been educated at a private school. But her parents had subjected her to a strict discipline and Natasha had become increasingly rebellious during her teens. Her rebellion had included taking drugs, and she had eventually run away from home and gone to live in a squat with other drug users.

Natasha had become friendly with the young man who supplied her with drugs. He also was young and good-looking, clean and tidy, unlike many of the people with whom she shared the squat. It was he whom we had also met with her that first night out on the streets. The deal was that he supplied her with drugs and she went out onto the streets to earn the money to feed them both. He even gave her a measure of protection by keeping his eye on her while she was out on her beat, and he was only doing his job when he accosted us. So he had become her pimp and her supplier, and she supported him financially in return. Natasha was eventually allocated a small terraced house in the city, where she lived alone but where she received visits from this boyfriend and from some of her clients. By now she had lost touch with her own family altogether.

Drugs absorbed her whole life. Many times during our acquaintance she would declare that she'd had enough of the life that she was living and would agree to start some course of treatment or rehabilitation, but when the time came she always refused to co-operate or to attend the centre; all her good resolutions would be swallowed up by the craving for drugs. We saw Natasha on the streets over a number of years and also visited her at her home. If we went to her house we would have to go in pairs because the effect of the drugs would sometimes make her violent. It was paying for the drugs that had driven her onto the streets in the first place and it was paying for the drugs that kept her there. We eventually lost touch with Natasha and I do not know what happened to her, but the prognosis for confirmed hard-drug users like her is not good.

Figures produced in 2007 by the National Christian Alliance on Prostitution suggest that as many as 95 per cent of the women working on the streets are using hard drugs like heroin or crack cocaine, and our experience in the Magdalene Group would bear that out. Drug abuse and the need to fund the habit is easily the commonest reason why girls go out onto the streets, and why they stay there.

◆　◆　◆

The children's charity Barnardo's made a video some years ago called *Whose Daughter Next?* The intention was to highlight the way in which very young girls can become trapped in prostitution. It tells the true story of a schoolgirl of 14 who is groomed by a man some eight or nine years older then her. She is frustrated, living at home with a mother who, she feels, still treats her like a child. She meets a young man who talks to her and takes her out for coffees. He flatters her and seems to admire her and treat her as an adult. He has money, sharp clothes and jewellery, and a flashy car. He is good-looking and all her school friends are envious of her relationship with him. She takes him home to meet her mother, who naïvely welcomes the friendship, even consenting to her daughter spending nights away at his flat. He buys her a ring and persuades her that he is serious about his relationship with her. By now she is pathetically in love with him.

Then he begins to cut her off from her friends and family, forbidding her to go home or contact her mother, or to phone her friends. If she disobeys him, he becomes violent and slaps and punches her. With a mixture of rewards for submission and threats and punishments for defiance, he gains control of her whole life. She becomes a willing victim, trying desperately to please him, terrified of losing him. She still thinks that she loves him, but it is a relationship of abject dependence on her side and total control on his.

One day he tells her that he is temporarily short of money and she can help him out by sleeping with a friend of his who will pay her for her services. And thus she becomes a prostitute. The abuse continues on an increasing scale as more and more men are brought to the house to use her. She feels disgusted and degraded by what she is being made to do, but her fear of losing the boyfriend is such that she will not refuse, and she cannot tell anyone else what is happening to her. When she goes to school she puts on a brave face and pretends that she is still enjoying the relationship. But she has been deliberately seduced and trapped into this way of life by a man who has already seduced and corrupted other girls before her and will move on in due course to seduce and corrupt others again.

In a study conducted in the Netherlands in 2000,[1] 79 per cent of the women who were interviewed said that their engagement in prostitution was due to some degree of force. This would include women who had been trafficked from other countries by organized criminals, often lured by spurious offers of legitimate employment but destined for a future as sex slaves. The schoolgirl in the Barnardo's video represents a form of entrapment much nearer to home but no less common. UK government figures[2] show that 75 per cent of such women lured into prostitution by this means become involved before the age of 18, and the average age for such initiation worldwide is 13–14. Of these, about a third will end up working on the streets, while the others will end up working in massage parlours, lap dancing clubs or escort agencies.

Such stories are not confined to girls or women. One of the cases that we encountered in the Magdalene Group was that of a young boy. We had originally gone to visit one of our female clients at her flat. It was in a house in which rooms were rented out to a variety of people. While we were there, our client asked us to go up to the attic. She was worried about a boy who lived up there who, she thought, was being pimped and who was not allowed to go out. My friend Toni and I went up the stairs and knocked quietly. 'Hi,' I said, through the closed door, 'my name is Theresa. Your friend downstairs asked us to knock and see if you were alright or if you needed some help.' A young voice said, 'Wait a minute.' When he opened the door and allowed us to come in, the sight and the smell were appalling. There was no furniture, not even a bed, just a filthy sleeping-bag in which he slept on the floor. There was nowhere for him or for us to sit down. There were no lights, and the room stank of urine and faeces.

It was his own father, he told us, who had got him this 'bedsit'. It was his father who was pimping him, taking money and sending men up throughout the day to abuse his own son. Men came from as far away as London for the 'pleasure' of sodomizing this young lad in these disgusting conditions. Hardened as we were becoming to stories of depravity, this was beyond belief. The boy was terrified of his father, too terrified to try to escape or to seek help. We reported his situation to the police and to social services immediately. I am glad to say that the father, who turned out to be a known sex offender of the worst sort, was arrested, tried, convicted and sent to prison. We encouraged the boy to come up and visit us at the Magdalene Group and we helped him to put some sort of a life together again. We were able to get him rehoused and to obtain furniture for him. It was difficult for him to come to terms with what had been done to him, and to this day he is in recovery from the traumas that he suffered.

Josephine, who we had first met through our street outreaches, was another woman who was involved in prostitution because of fear. She had been working the streets of Norwich for fourteen years and was controlled by a woman who pimped her. But the woman was the only face that she saw of an organized gang who would beat her up if she tried to step out of line and several times had inflicted grievous bodily harm on her. The gang was based in London but had women working for them in many different cities. Josephine had tried on several occasions to run away but the gang had always managed to track her down, she said, through the Benefits Agency. When we first met her we had given her a telephone number to ring if she was ever in danger again.

One evening she turned up at our drop-in centre, frightened out of her wits. She said that she could not even go back to her flat because there was a contract out on her life. By this time we had learned enough at the Magdalene Group to take this sort of threat seriously, so we contacted our friends in the vice squad. We had established a good relationship with these two police officers and they came over immediately to meet with Josephine. They also took her story seriously and arranged to spirit her out of the city that very night. The police themselves went to her flat and collected some clothes, unfortunately having to leave all her other possessions behind. Within an hour of Josephine coming in to our centre she was on the train out of Norwich to a safe house.

The National Women's Refuge is a body that co-ordinates the work of houses all over the country that offer sanctuary to abused and threatened women. Over the phone that night, NWR had located a room in a refuge in the north of England that would take Josephine in at short notice. Over the next few weeks, with the co-operation of the local police, Josephine changed her name and identity, changed her hair and her clothes, and with the support of the workers at the refuge timidly started to make a new life for herself. Josephine phoned us at the Magdalene Group from time to time to tell us how she was getting on. Eventually, she moved into a place of her own and started a college course. With a proper qualification she was able to find a job and establish a normal life. The last contact that we had with her was a Christmas card in which she thanked us again for all the help we had given her. The card ended with the words, 'I feel as free as a bird'. If drugs are the most common factor luring women into prostitution and keeping them there, then sheer brute force and fear is another.

Once we had learned that the girls who we met on the streets were more victims than vice girls, it would have been only too easy for us to go on to demonize the men and women who preyed on them and exploited them. Sometimes in our outreach on the streets and in our home visiting, we encountered some of these men for ourselves. Again, to our surprise, they did not turn out to be as threatening towards us as we thought they might be, even when we explained that we were offering the women help and support. One particular young man roared up on a motorbike while we were visiting one of our clients at home. This girl was a client of his too: he supplied her with drugs. He was disconcerted at first to meet us, but we started to talk to him and he began to tell us his own story. He was part of a gang who dealt in drugs and he, in turn, was frightened of what would happen to him if he tried to break away. He even wanted to know what we could do for him! He described his father as a prominent member of society and his mother as a 'do-gooder'. She, however, was also a secret alcoholic. His parents had beaten him as a child. One day he had come down to breakfast and told his mother that he felt sick and wanted to stay off school for the day. His parents would not listen to him and forced him to sit down and eat a bowl of porridge. Half way through his breakfast he was sick into the bowl. In spite of this his parents forced him not only to finish the porridge but also to eat his own vomit, and he was still sent to school. Physical and emotional abuse continued until the day when he could stand it no more and ran away from home. At 15 he found himself homeless and sleeping on the streets. He was picked up by an older man who sexually abused him, before falling in with the gang of drug dealers for whom he now worked. Truly this poor boy was as much a victim as the girl he was supplying.

It was not the remit of the Magdalene Group to take up cases like his, but I was able to refer this young man to another agency who offered him counselling and helped him to find a way out. We received Christmas cards from him for the next two years in which he reported the progress that he had made and his success at building a new life. We learnt to adopt a non-judgemental attitude even towards those who appeared to be the villains and abusers. 'Do not judge,' Jesus said, 'and you will not be judged.' We learnt over the years just how wrong we could be about the people we met. Many of them turned out to be more sinned against than sinning.

◆ ◆ ◆

In her book *Escaping the Devil's Bedroom*[3] Dawn Herzog Jewell identifies poverty as a major factor worldwide driving women into prostitution. 'Poverty is a significant "push factor" for women entering prostitution around the world. In Costa Rica, more than 27 per cent of the people live in poverty – a condition that frequently drives the market for children, who can bring in large sums of money at little cost to their pimps. The need for money results in families "pimping" their own children and leads women into the sex industry.' In Britain the safety net of the welfare state should mean that such desperate resorts are not necessary here. But the net does not catch everybody.

Illegal immigrants hoping to escape poverty in their countries of origin are unlikely to try to access the benefits system and are often virtually slaves to their traffickers. Many women today are caught in this trap, but few of them are let out onto the streets in case they escape; most will be working inside brothels.

One day, a couple of us from the Magdalene Group visited a young woman whom we had met on one of our outreaches. At home she had a little boy who was just about walking. When we arrived we saw that the toddler was wearing a black bin-liner in place of a nappy. The mother was afraid to go to the social services for fear that if they found out that she was working on the streets her little boy would be taken away from her and taken into care. We reassured her, and she agreed that we should contact social services on her behalf. They arranged for us to supply the woman with nappies and other things that she needed for the child. It was evident that the baby was loved, but this woman had been abandoned by the child's father and was now penniless. She had a serious drug habit on top of all her other troubles and she was afraid that she might harm her son while under the influence of drugs. But she wanted to change. We worked closely with social services and other agencies with this young woman for several years, and eventually she moved away to start a new life. Her poverty had been real, but unnecessary.

For Rachel, the third of the women who we had met on the streets on our first night of outreach, poverty was also real, relative to what other people might have. She worked as a prostitute only when she needed to top up her income. She was on state benefits, which meant that she was not destitute, but she did struggle to make ends meet. So if a particularly large bill came along or if she or her son needed to pay for something extra, like a school trip to France, then she would resort to selling herself. When I was a magistrate sitting on the bench, we had heard rumours that some of the students at the University of East Anglia were going out on the streets to supplement their student grants or loans. I never came across such girls in Norwich, but when I was researching the problem of prostitution in Norwich's twin city of Novi Sad in Serbia, I did meet girls who were using this as a way to earn the money to pay for university courses, either at home or abroad. Even in the developed world relative poverty can be a 'push factor' driving women onto the streets.

◆ ◆ ◆

As we heard more and more of the stories of these women we found that a common factor in their lives, like that of Cara, was often an experience of abuse when they were children. This would not be the only reason why they found themselves on the streets, but it seemed that it would often predispose them towards prostitution. Many of them, we found, had suffered physical or sexual abuse, bullying, even torture, either in the family home or at the hands of foster parents or 'carers' in institutions. Such experiences had invariably led to a sense of guilt and self-loathing. Such women have often, from an early age, been taught to regard themselves as scum. Other forms of domestic violence and broken family relationships can also induce in a child a false sense of guilt. All these negative emotions can lead to a girl putting no value on herself or her own body, and therefore predispose her to sell herself as something of little worth. The experience of being used by men in a casual and loveless way, accompanied as this often is by demands for the woman to co-operate in some sexual perversions, only confirm her in her low opinion of herself.

This is an inward and spiritual poverty that is much harder to see and to alleviate than the more obvious outward and material kind. It means a loneliness and an emptiness, a sense of not being whole, that is hard to understand for those who have never experienced it. In prostitution no woman stays whole. She becomes a commodity in the eyes of her customers and, in the end, in her own eyes too. Her namelessness and the dominance

and cruelty of the men, and sometimes the women, she
meets strip her of her identity. Surveys that have been
carried out by various agencies show consistently that 95
per cent of the women involved in prostitution hate
themselves and the way they live, and want to change
their lifestyle.

◆ ◆ ◆

Finally, women are sometimes on the streets because of
love – not the love of their customers but love for their
families or children. One of the most tragic cases that we
saw at the Magdalene Group was that of Hayley. She
came to us for help. She was quietly spoken, and if I had
seen her on the streets I would not have thought that she
was engaged in prostitution. I gave her a cup of coffee in
my office and she talked about her love for her mother
and her brother. She was trying to find accommodation
in Norwich that would enable her family to get back
together again. There was a history of trouble in the family. Her mother was an addict. Her mother's brother had
long since cut them off because he was disgusted at the
way his sister had encouraged her children, Hayley and
her brother, to start using drugs themselves. Hayley and
her mother had lived apart for several years. Hayley's
brother was currently in prison, though soon due for
release, and her mother was now ill and unable to care
for herself. When she came to the Magdalene Group,
Hayley was without food and hungry. She was working
on the streets to support her own drug habit and to raise
the money for a deposit on a house for them all to live in.

She was a sweet, kind girl, not yet hardened by the life
she led. Some of the other women who visited the drop-
in also knew Hayley and could only speak well of her
gentle nature. They were worried about her life on the

streets. She was very slight and often did not look well or strong. It was a dangerous place for such a slip of a girl.

We saw Hayley regularly over the next few months and were able to help her with some of her problems, including her housing problem. She and her mother moved into a new home and her brother came out of prison and joined them. Hayley was so happy that they could be a family again, but she still had to go out on the streets to feed them all and in particular to feed all three drug habits. I once asked Hayley what her mother thought of her daughter doing this for them. She said that her mother understood the necessity because she herself was too ill to take up any kind of work. Hayley had to make use of any means she could.

One day near Christmas in 2001, I went to their home with a hamper of food for the family. Denise, the mother, told me that she had not seen Hayley since one night back in October. Hayley had spent the evening in a local pub with a man she had met, and she had called in at home about midnight to say that she was going to stay out for the night with him. The man himself had come in to say hello and had assured Denise that he would take good care of her daughter, and he gave her the number of his mobile phone. That had been the last time that Denise had seen her daughter. It was not unusual for Hayley to stay away for a while with a man she had met, and so at first her mother had not been alarmed. But now two months had gone by and she was ready to go to the police and to report Hayley missing.

The police were able to trace the man through his mobile phone and the little white van that he had been using. He was called Philip Stanley, he lived in Essex and had a long criminal record of violence towards women. The police interviewed him, but he denied knowing

Hayley and denied being in Norwich at the time of her disappearance. However, when the police called to talk to him again a few days later, he had fled.

On 4 January, a woman walking her dog near the A3 at Petersfield in Hampshire discovered a shallow grave. In it the police found the decomposed body of our Hayley.

Stanley was tracked down, hiding under an assumed name in Ireland. He was eventually extradited and brought to justice in England. In 2005, Stanley was convicted of the murder of Hayley Curtis and sentenced to life imprisonment. This case, like that of the Ipswich girls, made national news. Like those cases, this one lifted the lid on the reality of prostitution and the tragic lives that are led by the women involved in it. Hayley once told me that she never wanted to go out on the streets and longed to have a normal family life. Knowing her gentle, loving nature I believe that she would have made a lovely wife and mother, if only she'd had the chance.

◆ ◆ ◆

When I first ventured out onto the streets I needed to know why the women were out there and what kept them there. I found out. It was not that they had considered a variety of career choices and decided upon this one. It was invariably a tale of poverty and abuse, of addiction, degradation and fear, beyond what most people could otherwise understand or imagine. There is no glamour or excitement about being out on dark streets on a cold night waiting to be picked up by a total stranger, taken to a lonely place and used in some disgusting way. It is an experience of abuse and exploitation, of powerlessness and loneliness.

I want to include here a poem written by one of the women we befriended at the Magdalene Group. It is a description of prostitution, not as fantasy, but as experienced by someone who knows the truth of it.

HELP

COLD
IT IS COLD
I AM COLD
As I stand in the gutter about to be sold,
Price tag not visible, that's all in my head,
It's a punter not lover that pays for my bed.

NUMB
I FEEL NUMB
I AM NUMB
As I work all the year, in snow, rain or sun,
Emotions closed off, yet I'm aware of my sins,
Not telling the punter the misery he brings.

LOST
I FEEL LOST
I AM LOST
I'm viewed as an object while my soul pays the cost.
He's buying my body with no care for my sanity.
I'm an actress pretending, while I lose my humanity.

SCARED
I FEEL SCARED
I AM SCARED
Prostitutes get killed and people don't care,
I'm a vulnerable woman alone in the dark,
Surrounded by sick men, the reality's stark.

TRAPPED
I FEEL TRAPPED
I AM TRAPPED
Like I've started a journey and there's no turning back,
Rent to pay, mouths to feed, and a habit to boot,
Addicted to fast money, existing on the loot.

HELP
I NEED HELP
I WANT HELP
To be free from the pain and self-loathing I've felt,
To lead a life of normality where sex is not sold
And I stand a good chance of growing gracefully old.

E.V.

There are ways out of the trap, but the women are rarely in a position to find a way out or take it by themselves. Their conditions have usually brought them to such a state of demoralization and despair that they lack the resources, material and spiritual, to lift themselves out of it. The prophet Jeremiah was once lowered into a deep and muddy pit as a punishment for speaking the word of the Lord. There was no way in which he could lift himself out. But friends came with old rags and a rope that they lowered down to him in his pit. He fastened the rags underneath his arms and his friends hauled him up on the rope out of the mire into a place of safety (Jer. 38:6–13). These women are in the same sort of pit, unable to save themselves. They need friends who will come alongside them and help them, encourage them to try, and support them as they rebuild their lives and follow their dreams. We were not always successful in doing this, but that is what the Magdalene Group was set up to do.

5

THE MAGDALENE GROUP

The Magdalene Group exists to encourage the spiritual, physical and educational well-being of people working within the sex industry and/or at risk of being involved in abusive or exploitative relationships. The aims of the Magdalene Group are to offer opportunities for change, if they so desire, and tackle issues of social exclusion by emancipatory approaches that develop the individual's self worth and confidence, in addition to providing preventative programmes and exit strategies.

That is how we described the aims and objects of the Magdalene Group when we set it up as a charitable trust. A group of Christians, including three magistrates, had recognized the growing social problem of women working in prostitution on the streets of Norwich, and had begun to pray that this problem would be addressed. When I heard God calling me, I had started going out on the streets at night with a small team of volunteers to meet the women there and find out more about their needs. The original prayer group, while continuing to pray, then became a sort of steering group to whom I reported back and with whom I could discuss our strategy. It quickly became clear that we needed a safe haven, open to anyone trapped in this lifestyle, where we could talk to them, build relationships of trust and address their personal issues, away from the streets where they worked and away from their often chaotic homes. We found suitable premises in the redundant church of St Peter Parmentergate and formed a charitable trust, thus becoming a legal entity that could raise and hold funds and enter into an agreement to lease and renovate the property.

At the beginning I was no more than the co-ordinator of the volunteers – at that time only three in number. When the trust was formed I became the manager of the project. While the work on the streets continued, I became the main fundraiser and the overseer of the building work. During this time I was still a volunteer, supporting myself and my family by working for various caring agencies. But as the project grew it became clear that we would have to raise the funds not only for the renovation of the building but also for a part-time salary for me. Over the next ten years we grew to the point where we employed seven paid staff which included me, a project co-ordinator, an operations manager, a pastoral worker, two support workers/volunteer co-ordinators and a schools worker. By this time I had become Director of the project, responsible for developing the vision and reporting on all our activities to the trustees.

One of my first jobs was to raise funds, and this remained an ongoing and arduous task, as anyone involved with charitable work will understand. We had no income-generating activities at all: our services were all freely given to our client group, who were only where they were because they needed money. Charging them for anything would have been self-defeating. So a large part of my life became applying for grants, making presentations and representing the Magdalene Group to dozens of bodies who might support our work. Once the rooms at St Peter's were open, the project began to attract interest from the local media, articles in the local papers and pieces on the regional television news. After that it became easier to get a hearing for our cause. We got money from businesses in the city like Norwich Union, John Lewis and Kettle Foods, from other charitable trusts both national and local, from individuals and from churches. In our 2004/2005 Annual Report we had a list of more than fifty sponsors who had helped to fund our work during that year. Sometimes we were able to get funding from government and other statutory bodies, like the local health authority, but this was often short term and always seemed to have too many strings attached to it. It was hard work applying for such funding and we could never rely on the outcome. For all these applications we had to produce a detailed and costed breakdown of our work and our plans and, if we were applying for a renewal of funding, we had to produce an evaluation of the results of our work so far. It was my responsibility, as Director, to put all these elements in place. It was here that my own experience in business really became an advantage. Later on, as the number of women using the centre increased, and as I became more and more involved with making sure that all our activities conformed to best practice, the trustees agreed to employ the services of a funding consultant with whom I could work.

At the heart of the work were our volunteers. We built up a team of more than thirty. Every Wednesday evening, from about 9 p.m. to midnight, a team of two women and one man would go out onto the streets in the red-light district to make contact with the women working there. The male volunteer was the driver and would normally stay in the car, waiting at a discrete distance. He was there to watch over the female volunteers in what can at any time become a frightening situation. They would go out, as we did at the beginning, armed with flasks of hot drinks, chocolate bars and free condoms for the girls to help prevent infections. They also took rape alarms to give to any of the women who wanted one. On any given night they might meet and talk to between five and twenty women, some of whom would be regular contacts. The job of the volunteers was to make new contacts, to gain a measure of trust from the women and to tell them about the ways in which the Magdalene Group was available to help them. If the girls did not already know about the Sitting Room, the volunteers would tell them about the services that we offered and invite them to call in and see us during the day.

The Sitting Room was also manned by a rota of volunteers. It was open three days a week – Monday, Wednesday and Friday – from about midday to late afternoon. There would be a volunteer always ready to welcome the women who dropped in and to offer them a drink and a chat. There were always sandwiches and homemade cakes to eat, and everything was free. Downstairs there was a shower with clean, fluffy, white towels, and we always kept a supply of clean underclothes to give the girls if they needed them. On a Wednesday evening we were open for hot dinners, and these became social events, with many of the girls coming in to eat and spend time with friends before going out onto the streets. These were times for laughter and fun in lives that were all too often devoid of both, and sometimes quite serious discussions would occur in which the women would talk about their thoughts and feelings and beliefs in a way in which perhaps they had never done before. Over the years we built up a clientele of more than two hundred women with whom we were working at some level of engagement.

Although we had set up the Magdalene Group primarily with the problem of street prostitution in mind, we also found that other women in the city who were working in nightclubs and massage parlours began to contact us. The word spread amongst those working in the wider sex industry that our services were available and that we were a non-judgemental source of help.

Part of my responsibility was the recruitment and training of our volunteers. Almost all came from local churches. I would receive an invitation to speak about the Magdalene Group at a church meeting or a church service, and I would set out our needs both for funding and for volunteers. Anyone who came forward would be asked to complete an application form. From this we could build up a picture of the volunteer, their reasons for offering their time and any skills or experience that they might have that would be valuable to our girls. We always asked for two references, including one from their minister or priest. I would then arrange to interview each volunteer at the drop-in centre and show them something of our work first hand.

Those whom we agreed to accept and those who still wanted to volunteer after what they had seen and heard were then put on a three-month training programme. At this time there were only one or two similar projects of this sort in the UK, and we had to set up the systems for running it from scratch. The volunteers received training in listening skills, and teaching on health issues, drug awareness, and the law, and some of these were given by other agencies on our behalf: the police, the drug clinics and the health service. During these three months our new volunteers would also shadow a more experienced helper, doing outreach on the streets at night, attending sessions at the Sitting Room, and visiting clients in their homes with our pastoral worker. Not all our volunteers lasted the course: some decided that this was not their scene after all and dropped out, but others became the backbone of our work.

Many of our volunteers were older women who had brought up families of their own and now had time to give. Sometimes we had younger girls who were studying at the University of East Anglia. Their work at the Magdalene Group would in some cases be counted as a placement on their courses, and some of these young women were splendid and went on to make a career in similar projects elsewhere in the country. But one of our outstanding volunteers was a very mature lady called Janet. One evening, a woman we knew well, Diane, dragged herself into my office very late at night. She had been viciously raped by a customer. She was bruised and bleeding and was covered in dog mess, even matted in her hair, but she had made her way back to our centre in the hope of finding help. I immediately reached for the phone and asked Janet if she could come down and help me comfort this poor girl. So at 11 p.m., 87-year-old Janet drove through the dark streets of Norwich to our drop-in. In spite of her age Janet could go into any situation and be unruffled. She had brought with her some silk pyjamas and a pair of slippers for Diane. We made her a hot drink and listened to her tale. We offered her a shower, which she gratefully took, and shampooed the dog mess out of her hair. We encouraged her to report the rape to the police, but she adamantly refused to do so. She did not even want to tell her partner about what had happened to her, and if the police were involved it would inevitably come out. We marvelled at the depravity of what many of these women suffered from the men around them, but were grateful that Diane had at least been able to find some love and understanding through Janet and me.

For all such and a variety of other situations I had to write policies and procedures. It sounds excessively bureaucratic but it was important. It was important for the safety and well-being of our staff and volunteers; it was important for the safety and well-being of the women themselves; and it was important that we should be able to show the world that our work was above reproach if any accusations of misconduct should arise. There is a mountain of legislation these days governing health and safety, the protection of children and vulnerable adults, and governing data protection and confidentiality. Into all this our volunteers and staff had to be thoroughly inducted and we had to have clear guidelines and rules that made sure that we were compliant with all these regulations. Through it all, we tried hard to keep this in the background for the women whom we befriended and served. For them, we wanted the Sitting Room to be a home not an institution, and we wanted to be their friends not their social workers. So we ourselves knew the rules and the procedures, but we did not put them up on the walls. Perhaps because we had all these safeguards in place, none of our workers was ever assaulted, threatened or sued. We had to have soft hearts and hard heads.

There were, of course, some rules and procedures that the women did have to know and understand. The Sitting Room had to be a drug-free zone. While we understood that many or most of them were addicted, neither using nor dealing drugs nor drinking alcohol on our premises could be tolerated. From time to time someone had to be excluded from the Sitting Room for breaking this rule. But we never made exclusion permanent: there was always a door open for repentance and a fresh start. We could hardly claim to be Christian if we did not believe in the possibility of redemption for even the most flagrant of sinners. People also had to understand that if we became aware, through our work, of children at risk, and many of our clients had children at home, then we had to inform the social services or the police, whatever agreements about confidentiality we had made with the women themselves.

Once the staff grew beyond Toni, our pastoral worker, and me, we had to keep careful, confidential records of our engagement with each woman. When they first came into the drop-in centre or asked for our help we would encourage them to sit down with one of us and take them through an assessment form. I would ask about their health, addictions, their finances, their involvement with other agencies, their relationships with partners, children, families and the history of their involvement in prostitution. This would help me to build up a picture of the woman's life and of her needs. When people seek help they often present a fairly trivial need that cloaks much deeper and more persistent problems. For example, a woman might come simply asking for food for herself and her child, but underneath there would be a story of debt, of drug or alcohol abuse, of bad health, perhaps of a man or a woman living on her immoral earnings. To give her the food she needed immediately was the easy bit; encouraging her to tackle her deeper problems might involve us all in years of hard work. But this assessment was always voluntary. If a woman declined to tell us anything more about herself we always respected her right to privacy and never pressed the issue until she was ready.

In the Sitting Room was a day book, in which the volunteers on duty wrote down the names of all the people who came to the room and a record of any need of which they became aware. In addition, the volunteers had report forms on which they passed through to the office any requests for help, for home visits, or for any of the services that we were able to offer. We aimed to operate a 'one-stop shop': to be a place where a woman could come with any request or need and we would either meet it ourselves or refer her to another agency or source of help. We were not in the business of sending people away to seek help elsewhere. These women were often grievously lacking in self-confidence and self-respect. They might have come to trust us, but part of their problem was that they were not good at dealing with officials, with benefit officers, housing officers, children's workers, policemen, or even doctors and nurses. They were likely to become confused or aggressive, which would not help their case. Where it was necessary to send someone on to one of these agencies, one of us always went with them.

We were also concerned to know what the women thought of the services that we provided. About once every six weeks we would have an open meeting in the Sitting Room to which anyone could come and at which we invited people to have their say. We called these meetings 'The Voices' and sometimes they gave us valuable ideas about new ways in which we could develop the work and extend the help that we offered.

It was not long before our facilities at St Peter Parmentergate became inadequate. First, I needed a dedicated office from which to work. A desk in the corner of the Sitting Room was simply too public. We had to keep records that were highly confidential and there was nowhere secure to store them. Telephone calls came in at all hours of the day and night, especially after we installed a 24-hour helpline, and it was not possible to conduct confidential telephone conversations in a busy

Sitting Room. So when a small printer's office down the street became available we took over the rental and I moved the paperwork and the administration down there. We were also coming to recognize that education and training must be a priority in our efforts to help women who wanted to exit this lifestyle. Few of them had done well at school or gone on to higher education and most were sadly lacking in the sort of skills needed in the workplace. The girls did not only need to stop earning money on the streets, they needed to be equipped to earn money in some other way. At least in the early stages, we would have to offer this sort of education and training on our own premises, before ever our clients would be able to access the facilities in the city. So a few years later we found another room where we could build up our educational activities which were being taken up by more and more of our clients. Even with these additions to our facilities we were soon running out of space again, and in 2003 we moved across the road from St Peter Parmentergate into new premises that housed a new drop-in centre and administrative base. We kept on the rooms at St Peter's and in the old printer's office, which gave us greater flexibility in responding to the needs of individuals and groups.

At the heart of our work, and in the hearts of our staff and volunteers, was our belief that God loved each person that we met, and that with his love and our love and help they could achieve lasting change in their lives, if they wanted to do so. But we could only help those who were willing to help themselves. If our work was to bear any fruit, a woman had to want to change. Most of them did, but change almost always involved a prolonged commitment on their part and on ours. There were rarely quick fixes for the multiple and deep-rooted problems that most of the girls had. Some were able to make that commitment and to persevere through the hardships; others, sadly, were not. But we never gave up hope for each one. Sometimes it was years before we saw a woman make any progress towards the goals that she had set herself.

The whole project had been birthed in prayer and continued to be bathed in prayer. My own calling to this work had come out of a commitment to doing the will of God in my life, and without a constant reliance on God in prayer I do not believe that I could have sustained that commitment through nearly sixteen years. Many were the times when I would say to someone, 'Just wait a moment while I go away for a few minutes,' and I would retreat to my office to pray. The staff and I and any of our volunteers who were available held regular prayer meetings. Just as we recognized that lasting change could not come about without the active co-operation of the women themselves, so we recognized that lasting change could not come about without the work of God's Holy Spirit. We could do all that was humanly possible but, as Jesus said, without him and without the help of his Holy Spirit we could do nothing. Only God could reach into the hearts and minds of these broken bodies and souls and touch them in a way that would make a lasting difference.

We had a Quiet Room at the drop-in centre, where anyone could go to be alone, to pray if they wanted to, or simply to cuddle up under a blanket. When Janet, our 87-year-old volunteer, died, the women themselves got together and bought a statue of an angel to put in the Quiet Room in memory of her. There were Bibles in the Quiet Room given to us by the Gideons. On Wednesday evenings Toni, our pastoral worker or one of the volunteers would lead a Bible study with some of the women. They would take a few verses from the Bible and each would say what these verses meant to them. The girls were astonished to find that they were in the Bible themselves. As well as the story of the woman of the streets who came to Jesus in the house of Simon the Pharisee, they found the story of Rahab the harlot in Jericho who gave a friendly welcome to the Israelite spies (Joshua 2), and they were astonished when they read that Jesus said to the Pharisees, 'The tax-collectors and the prostitutes are entering the kingdom of God ahead of you' (Matthew 21:31). Most of the women would know that we prayed for them because we often told them so, and they knew that they could always ask for prayer, and sometimes they did.

Thus, from the outset, the Magdalene Group had a distinctively Christian ethos, an ethos that we were determined to maintain. It was not just that the inspiration and motivation for our work came from our own experience of the love of God, nor just that we looked at all times to the power of God to do what we could not do, but also that we tried to make sure that our Christian convictions informed all our relationships. We believed that everyone was precious in the sight of God, and therefore we had to treat everyone with care and respect. We believed that this should condition our relationships not only with the men and women who we met on the streets, but also our relationships with one another, as trustees, staff and volunteers. These things should, and I believe do, make a Christian organization different from a secular or non-Christian one.

We had to bear all this in mind when we were required by new government legislation in 2003 to define our distinctively Christian ethos and justify the employment of explicitly Christian staff or volunteers. When advertising for a salaried member of staff we had to ask ourselves whether a Christian commitment was a 'genuine occupational requirement' for the post. This was a difficult exercise. Sometimes we did employ both staff and volunteers who were not Christians but who were happy to work within our Christian ethos. We also had some volunteers who were over eager to bring God into every encounter and every conversation. One in particular gave us all spiritual indigestion, and we had to take her aside and explain the way we worked before she alienated too many of our clients. On the other hand, we once had an application from a person who declared herself to be a Satanist. At interview we explained the central place that Christian prayer had in our life together and asked her if she would be happy to work in such an environment. She withdrew her application.

None of this applied to our clientele. We were committed to helping our client group without discrimination on the grounds of ethnicity, religion, disability or sexual orientation. We made no enquiries at all about the women's beliefs or spiritual state. There was no requirement or expectation that they should be or even want to become Christians. We existed to provide them with any help that they wanted with no strings attached. If someone wanted to know about our God or about what made us tick as Christians, then we were happy to tell them more, but we never forced such a conversation upon anyone. In fact, many of our girls talked quite freely to us about God; a surprising number of them had had some experience of angels. But we were clear that we were not an evangelistic organization. We were there to express the love of God in action.

In spite of that, some of the men and women who came to us did become Christians. They experienced the love of God in our Sitting Room and in the way that we loved them. Some of them were enabled to pick up the threads of Christian teaching that they had received in childhood and make this the basis of a new start. Of course we rejoiced whenever we saw this happen. We knew that only in a relationship with God would they find the self-worth that so many of them lacked. Only at the Cross of Christ would they find the forgiveness of their sins and cleansing and release from the guilt and defilement that clung to them so closely. Only in the power of the Holy Spirit could they find the strength to resist the temptations of the world from which they were trying to escape. Nevertheless, we could help them, step by step, to reorder their lives and leave their present lifestyle, even if they did not come to share our faith and knowledge of Jesus our Saviour.

If a woman did want to become a Christian we would try to link her up with one of the local churches. We were equally clear that the Magdalene Group was not a church. In a local church the woman would be taught and nurtured and, we hoped, be surrounded by a loving, accepting fellowship, such as she had found at the Magdalene Group. This was not always easy. I once took such a young woman along to the woman's local church. At the end of the service she made a sharp exit, whispering in my ear, 'I can't go back there again.'

'Why not?' I asked.

'Because the vicar was one of my customers,' she said.

It was indeed true that the men who used our clients' services came from every walk of life, from illegal immigrants working in the fields, to businessmen, lawyers, even judges, policemen and, yes, vicars.

Such a story, however, was not typical. The Magdalene Group enjoyed the support and encouragement of most of the churches in the city and the surrounding area. Amongst our patrons we were able to count both the Anglican Bishop of Norwich and the Roman Catholic Bishop of East Anglia. And when it came to supporting our girls some of these churches were wonderful. They received them and welcomed them, loved them and helped them in every way. As these women grew into their new freedom in Christ and found new friends, we often lost touch with them at the Magdalene Group. That was fine by us – the doctor does not expect his patients to keep in touch with him once they are well. But from time to time we might hear from a minister in the city or from some other Christian friend how well a former client was doing. Then, our cup was full.

6

MEETING IMMEDIATE NEEDS

A day in the life of Jodie, one of the Magdalene Group's support workers:

My day starts at 8.30 a.m. as I arrive at a client's flat to take her to the hospital for an anti-natal check-up. She is called Melanie. We arrive at the hospital and take our seats in the waiting room. When her number is called we go through for the ultrasound, but she cannot bring herself to look at the screen as she has just been told that the baby will be taken away from her shortly after birth. Life has been a real struggle for this woman and she has found herself in an existence of drugs and prostitution. Although she has tried hard to conquer her addictions and mental health problems, it has not been easy and social services have decided that it is best for the baby to be placed in care.

When I arrive at the office I pick up my messages, make some support calls and make a start on my paperwork. One of the calls is to a young lady, Vanessa, who is currently going through a home detox to come off her methadone script. She is doing really well and has a positive attitude towards it, which is great to hear.

At 12.30 p.m. I don my big thick rubber gloves to pick up two used needles that have been discarded outside the project door.

At 1 p.m. the drop-in session starts and the volunteers arrive for the afternoon. I give them a brief update and share any operational issues that may be relevant. The first client arrives and the volunteers make her a cup of tea and a toasted ham and cheese sandwich.

A little later on a girl turns up at the door who is not known to us. She is crying and asking for help. After getting her a drink and something to eat I do an initial assessment. She tells a familiar story of abuse, drugs and homelessness. I listen and try to work out how we can be of the most help to her. I then make appointments for her to see other relevant agencies that might be able to help her. After ringing around various hostels we are unable to find her a bed for the night. She says that she will return to the shed where she has been sleeping for the past few weeks. We provide her with a food parcel and some warm clothes to keep her going. I arrange for her to come back to the project the next morning to continue the search for a bed space.

At 5 p.m. I head for home and deliver a food parcel on the way. One of the clients contacted us earlier in the day saying that she had nothing to eat and no money to get anything until the following week. Unfortunately, however, due to her chaotic lifestyle she is not in when I arrive, so I put a note through her door and will try to deliver it again in the morning.

Jodie was one of the young women who came to us as a volunteer whilst she was studying at the University of East Anglia. After she graduated she became a member of our staff. Such a day as this reveals something of the spectrum of needs that the Magdalene Group existed to meet. They range from the immediate need for food to the much longer-term need for treatment for drug addiction and mental illness, from the physical need for shelter to the deeper emotional need of a woman losing her child. These needs were rarely neatly isolated or self-contained, but were more often all tangled up together. However, we could only tackle these needs by dealing with them one by one.

Food was often the most basic need. A few of the people with whom we came into contact were simply destitute but more often the need for food was drug-related. For an addict, drugs or drink come before food as a claim on the personal budget and, worse still, drugs or drink often come before the children's food as a claim on the family budget. The cravings are so acute that anything can be sacrificed to paying for the next fix. We never gave out money that we knew would only too quickly be spent on drugs. We would sometimes purchase top-up cards for the electricity or gas meter out of our contingency fund, but we never gave anyone money.

We frequently gave food. We kept stocks of non-perishable items on our own premises. These were used to feed our clients when they came to the drop-in centre, and to cater for the Wednesday evening dinners. Our volunteers often brought cakes and other items that they had baked at home for these occasions too. We could pack up a food parcel at any time for a woman or a family whose cupboards were bare. Somehow or other God saw to it that our own cupboards were never bare but were always well stocked with good things. We never knew of women who took advantage of this generous provision; they only asked us for food when they were in dire need. We never had to refuse a request for food for any reason. Donations of food items would come in to us from churches in the city and round about, from Women's Institutes and Mothers' Unions, and from other groups and individuals who had heard about our work and our needs. When I went out speaking about the work of the Magdalene Group, the attitudes of people towards the women on the streets were often so radically changed that they would ask what they could do to help, and one of the things that they could do was to give us food.

We made a particular point of distributing food at Christmas time. We made up hampers full of treats for the women and their children. As well as food for the family, we would go out and buy nice smelly soaps and perfumes for the women, and games and toys for the children. One year Bernard Matthews, the well-known Norfolk poultry firm, gave us thirty-two oven-ready turkeys. At other times Marks & Spencer gave us vouchers with which to purchase extra Christmas goodies. A group of women in the churches of North Norfolk baked lovely Christmas cakes for us each year. Our staff and volunteers were greeted with such excitement when they went to deliver these hampers, especially by the children, who might otherwise have got little or nothing in the way of extras for the festive season. Some of the recipients were overwhelmed by the generosity of strangers: 'Who are these lovely people,' they would ask, 'who have given us all this, when they don't even know us?' We could only tell them that for the most part they were Christians in the local churches who wanted to show them that God loved and cared for them: he had given them these lovely hampers but, best of all, he had given them Jesus.

◆　◆　◆

When we first contacted our clients on the streets we often found that they had no stable housing arrangements. They might be dossing down in a squat, or sleeping on the sofa or the floor of a friend's flat. They might be sleeping rough under the staircase in one of the multi-storey car parks or at the back of the railway station. Even those with a bedsit or a flat of their own might be facing eviction for non-payment of the rent.

We often found clients, who had been sleeping rough, on our doorstep early in the morning when we came to work. They would be cold and tired and hungry. We would take them up to the Sitting Room, make them a hot drink and hot buttered toast, and they would have a shower and a change of clothes. One morning one of our rough sleepers arrived early at my office door. She was a girl we knew well, but she looked exhausted and ill. She had spent the night in hospital. One of her fingers had been chopped off by her drug dealer because she had tried to steal his mobile phone. The hospital had sewn her finger back on and discharged her back onto the streets. We took her in, made a fuss of her and encouraged her to talk about her situation. We told her that if she wanted to change her way of life, we would help her, but the decision had to be hers. We would always be there for her if she wanted to quit.

There was an acute shortage of accommodation for homeless women in the city. The number of beds in the hostels was never sufficient and some of the hostels would not take women who were addicted to drugs or to alcohol, which accounted for most of our clients. Usually our first thought when we were trying to find a bed for a woman on the streets was to ask if she had any friends or relatives who might take her in for just twenty-four hours. In the meantime we could be busy on the telephone looking for somewhere more permanent for her. We would help her to fill in an application form for the city's housing department. We would accompany her to an interview with a housing officer and the benefits agency. The presence and advocacy of one of our experienced staff was often crucial in getting the woman accommodation. The women themselves were often fearful and volatile in such situations and given to outbursts that did not help their cases. Also, there was an element of prejudice against our clients when it came to the allocation of housing, which our staff could sometimes confront. Where there was a history of the woman having been a bad tenant with rent arrears in the past, we could undertake to work out a scheme of weekly payments that would clear off her arrears and enable her to keep up her payments in the future. As the city's housing department came to know and trust the Magdalene Group, we found it easier to arrange suitable accommodation for our clients. But only too often we discovered that their chaotic lifestyles had lost them golden opportunities to establish a more settled way of life.

Once a client was assured of a tenancy, we then tried to help her to make a real home there. Sometimes they were starting with nothing. Social services might make a grant or a loan for basic items such as a cooker, a fridge, a kettle and some bedding. But the money was never enough to furnish a flat. We would put out an appeal to our volunteers and their churches for items of furniture, rugs and curtains, pots and pans, cups and saucers and, perhaps, help with redecorating a room or two.

This all became much easier once the Besom became established in the city. The Besom is another Christian organization that started work in London in 1987 and has since spread to other parts of the country. It aims to be a bridge between those who want to give and those in need. Those who want to give may want to give time or money or goods, and the Besom can use them all to make a difference to the lives of people, such as the women with whom we worked. The Besom was run by Christians from a number of city churches. We would ring them and tell them that one of our women was ready to move into a new house or flat and give them a list of her needs. The Besom does not recycle junk. The pieces of furniture that they would offer a woman would all be in excellent condition, and she would be able to see what she was being offered and decide whether to accept it or reject it before it was delivered to her. People may be poor, but the Besom treats them with respect and gives them the dignity of choice: foisting unwanted goods onto them does neither. So, later, we could turn to the Besom with our client's needs and know that they would provide for them anything that they had in a sensitive and caring way.

Over the years we established a track record with the city housing department, not only in helping women into suitable accommodation, but also in supporting them in it afterwards. This record was recognized when the city council agreed to pay for two additional members of staff for us as floating support workers. These two workers were funded to go on supporting our clients in managing their finances, paying their rent and other domestic utilities, and looking after their property as good tenants. Just as we had always aimed to make our own Sitting Room a model of comfort and cleanliness, so we encouraged the women to take a pride in their own homes. This in turn gave them greater self-respect. They could invite their own friends and neighbours round for a coffee without feeling ashamed of their surroundings. Some of these women had been used to living in squalor, even from childhood. When Toni and I started to visit them in their homes we were shocked at the poverty and very often the filth that we encountered. When people have lost their self-respect they cease to care about their surroundings either: kitchens full of dirty dishes and the remains of uneaten food; children playing round unemptied potties; discarded needles that had been used for injecting heroin left lying on the sofa. In the end, housing was not merely a matter of shelter and safety, though God knows the streets were a dangerous and miserable place to live, but a nice home was an achievement, especially for a woman, and a great step forward towards feeling an equal member of society and not an outcast.

One of the women we helped in this way was Sophie. She was referred to us from the Bure Centre, a drug rehabilitation unit run by the county council. She already knew some of the other women at the Magdalene Group. She was due to be discharged after detoxing, but had nowhere to go and no possessions to speak of. Social services found her a tenancy and gave her a crisis loan. Meanwhile, we supported her in her application to the benefits agency, and we were able to obtain clothes for her, furniture, bedding and other household necessities. As she settled down, she continued to come into our Sitting Room and began attending our craft sessions, where she made new friends and discovered new skills. She also became a Christian and started to attend a chapel in the town that gave her much support and encouragement.

◆   ◆   ◆

I remember well the first time I appeared again in court – this time to speak on behalf of one of the women. The day came when I had to accompany one of our clients to the magistrates' court to face a charge of non-payment for her television licence. She was called Tess. At the age of 14 she had had a row with her parents and had left home to live on the streets of Manchester. She had been picked up by a 40-year-old man who had taken her home to his flat, befriended and spoiled her. It was a classic case of an unscrupulous older man grooming a young and vulnerable girl for prostitution. After a few weeks he began to bring other men to the flat to have sex with her. The final step was to drive her out to work on the streets. Over several years she had had two children, and was pregnant with a third when she had fled from this man and come to Norwich. When she first came to the Magdalene Group she was working from home and penniless. She had heard about us from other women working on the streets and was looking for help and a way out of prostitution. She was also afraid that her ex-partner and pimp would find her and punish her for running away.

Beside all this, non-payment of her TV licence was a small matter, but accompanying her to court and telling the court something of her circumstances and her efforts to change her lifestyle was just one of the ways that we could support Tess and encourage her. Our friends in the vice squad were very co-operative in arranging for her to summon help quickly if she were threatened by her ex-pimp, and step by step we were able to help her overcome her problems and make a life for herself and for her children in which she did not need to sell her body to make ends meet. In the end, she was able to move back to Manchester and was reunited with her family.

The women who came to the Magdalene Group were often up before the courts on one charge or another: soliciting obviously, non-payment of fines or television licences, theft, shoplifting, possession of drugs, or occasionally some sort of assault or affray. I had known from the beginning that I should be alongside these women, supporting them and perhaps speaking for them. But I had to be careful. I never advertised the fact in the Magdalene Group that I had once been a Justice of the Peace, but once the women knew of my judicial past, some would quickly jump to the conclusion that I could pull strings for them or otherwise persuade the magistrates to be lenient. Of course, that was never in my mind.

One of our workers would often accompany a woman to her court appearance just to make sure that she arrived to answer the charge and to encourage her afterwards to deal with the outcome. If I knew the full facts of the case, I would sometimes go to court to present any mitigating circumstances or ask for a particular judgement as being the most appropriate. I could use my knowledge of the law and of the options open to the court in this way without compromising my integrity or showing partiality. I would always consult beforehand with any solicitors, probation officers or social workers involved in the case, so that we could co-ordinate our representations to the bench. I could sometimes vouch for the fact that a woman was seriously trying to change her way of life and was working with us at the Magdalene Group to sort out her problems. A custodial sentence might set back the efforts that we had all made over many months, not least the woman herself, whereas a suspended sentence or a Community Service Order might give us all more time to keep up the good work that had been begun. I am glad to say that the magistrates were often sympathetic to such cases and dealt with them with mercy as well as justice. In due course, the magistrates themselves came to recognize the value of the Magdalene Group and would sometimes refer women arrested for soliciting on the streets to us for help.

In all these ways we continued to value the opportunities that we had to work together with other agencies, both voluntary and statutory. We always found that multi-agency support was better than one of us trying to do it all alone. In time, the Magdalene Group itself came to be recognized by other agencies as a valuable partner in our own field.

The most heartbreaking hearings that I ever had to attend were those in the family courts where a judge had to make a decision on whether or not to remove a child from its mother or parents. This was, and is, the most difficult area of the law for everyone concerned. It was often not a question of criminal behaviour on the part of the woman or her partner, though sometimes of course it was, but it might simply be the woman's inability, because of her addictions or other health problems, to look after her children properly. To take a child into care, to offer it for adoption, to put it out to foster parents or into a children's home away from its mother, is a traumatic decision for everyone. Neither the social workers nor the judges can ever be sure that they are doing the right thing. None of the courses of action open to them are ideal: the best is only the best of a bad job. Sometimes the courts and social services make spectacular mistakes, either in leaving a child with its natural parents or in removing it. They can find themselves pilloried in the popular press and turned into figures of hate. But the situations with which they are dealing are always bad ones to start with, and they can only do their best to make things better.

As this area of our work increased, I trained other workers on our staff and amongst our volunteers to undertake this sort of advocacy. The support that we were able to give sometimes made all the difference between a child being able to stay with its mother, and the mother and child being separated. But the woman that Jodie was supporting at the beginning of this chapter was a tragic case. Melanie had been in and out of mental hospital and had wanted to stay in hospital whilst she was waiting for the birth of her baby. She was now being treated at home with methadone to wean her off her addiction to heroin, but she was struggling with her psychological issues and from time to time she relapsed. A child protection conference had recently taken place and, although the professionals concerned had recognized the effort that Melanie was making to overcome her problems, they had decided that the baby should be placed on the Child Protection Register and would probably be taken into care.

In the remaining weeks before the baby was due, the case seemed to swing one way and then the other. Melanie continued to try very hard to resist the temptation to use heroin, and still had hopes of being able to keep the child if she did well enough. However, the baby was born addicted to methadone and had to remain in hospital after the birth. Melanie was emotionally torn: on the one hand she loved this little bundle as every mother does, and wanted to spend as much time with her baby as possible; on the other hand, she was frightened of becoming too close to the child in case she was going to lose her. Mother and baby both seemed to be doing well for a while, and Melanie was hopeful that she and the baby would be allowed to go together into a rehabilitation unit. But at a final case conference social services decided that they could not fund this: the mother might go into rehabilitation by herself, but the baby would be taken into care. Melanie was devastated. She had by now bonded closely with the child, and it transpired that she did not have the will to resolve her own difficulties if there was no child to look after. She went into rehab but did not stay long. Coming out she went back on drugs and went back on the streets. Eventually we lost touch with her.

It is easy to think that the professionals were wrong to do this, that funding considerations came before the welfare of this mother and child. But who knows? At the Magdalene Group we knew of cases where the birth of a child had been exactly the stimulus that a woman needed to sort her life out, kick her drug habit, come off the streets and start a new life. But sadly that did not always happen, and who knows whether this decision was not better for Melanie's baby in the long run. But I think that Melanie's heart was finally broken, and Jodie's was too. There are no easy answers.

◆ ◆ ◆

Entwined with all these problems so often was a chronic inability to manage money. Drugs demand money, lots of it. The reason many of the women were out on the streets in the first place was to make enough money to fund their addictions. Drugs came before food, rent, the electricity bill, and even the children's food and clothing. Women would often resort to other means of raising money to fill the gaps, like theft or shoplifting. If they were caught and prosecuted they might face custodial sentences that would cause yet more grief and heartache for mothers and children alike. And so the cycle of trouble and despair would repeat itself. If any order or stability was to be introduced into the lives of these women, one of the immediate needs was for them to get a grip on their finances. This was not always the same thing as coming off the streets or changing their way of life. Even in their existing circumstances it was still possible to encourage them to control their debts.

It is difficult to overestimate the extent to which the lives of the women were controlled by fear. They were afraid of men, often with good reason; they were afraid of drug dealers; they were afraid of the police; they were afraid of almost anyone in authority; they were afraid of social workers who might take their children away; they were afraid of threatening letters coming through the door with final demands for the payment of their bills. Such letters were often not even opened but stuffed down the side of the settee or even thrown away. But they could have their electricity or gas cut off or be evicted by the landlord. One of the ways that we could help them at the Magdalene Group – and that I in particular could help them through my experience in business and accountancy – was to sort out their finances.

Many of the women had never had any guidance or teaching in how to manage a budget. I remember my own mother in the East End of London who unconsciously taught me how to manage money. She had different tins or jars into which she put the money for different bills as she got it from her own and Dad's wages: so much for food, so much for the rent, so much for the children's clothes, so much for a rainy day. I would pass on these homely tips to our girls and encourage them to adopt some modern version of this form of budgeting. We never challenged our clients about where they chose to spend their money; it was their money and they had to take responsibility for deciding how to spend it. It required endless patience to persevere with them through their relapses into foolish and profligate spending, but in the end it often worked.

When they were already facing a mountain of debt, I would say, 'Find a black plastic bin-bag and fill it up with all the unpaid bills, the unopened letters and the papers that you don't understand, and bring it in to me.' I would then sort it all out for them and work out exactly where they stood, how much was owed and to whom. I would then offer to write to all their creditors and arrange terms for the payment of their debts. If she was willing, the girl would sign a letter appointing me to be her agent and I would then approach the companies and people to whom she was in debt with a reasonable plan to pay off the arrears. Presented with a realistic plan of this sort, most corporate bodies will settle for the incremental payment of a proportion of the debt, often being willing to remit a part of it in return for regular and sustained contributions. As a last resort I would apply to the courts for an administration order. Sometimes it is the only alternative to losing the whole amount as a bad debt. The benefits agency will also co-operate in paying some debts of this sort by transferring direct to the creditor a sum from the client's benefits, thus removing the temptation for the client to buy drugs instead of paying the gas bill.

◆ ◆ ◆

In amongst all this we also managed to have some fun together, fun being something that was often sorely lacking in these women's lives. As well as our weekly dinner parties at the Sitting Room, one of our volunteers would take a group of them swimming at the local swimming-pool. In the summertime we arranged family outings for the women and their children, for a picnic or a day at the seaside. It was amazing to see how such simple things could give back to these women a sense that they were normal people doing normal things like everyone else, and not pariahs, shunned by the rest of society.

◆ ◆ ◆

One of the jobs that the Magdalene Group's support worker, Jodie, recorded for the day with which we began this chapter, was a telephone call to Vanessa, coming off her methadone. This is Vanessa's own story:

My name is Vanessa; I'm now 32 years old. I became a Christian when I was 12 years old. As a child I was abused very badly and nobody ever believed me until one day a teacher at my school asked me why I was always so sad. I trusted this lady and told her. My mother knew, but was also afraid to do anything.

As I grew older I began to fall away from the Lord and get in with the wrong crowd of people, and I started to take drugs. Then one day I got raped. It was then that I decided to go out onto the streets and sell my body for money. At the time I thought, I may as well do that rather than be used and abused. Also by this point I needed the money.

Then one night I met Jodie when they were out helping girls. That was the turning point in my life. I've now been clean from street drugs for nineteen months. I'm back in Christian fellowship and right now as I write this I'm on day seven of a home detox from methadone. I've not had any for four days.

I would like to say a big, big thank you to Toni and Jodie from the Magdalene Project for helping me to get this far, and for all their valuable support and care. Neither of them ever doubted me, which also means a great deal to me, and they have never judged me or thought bad of me.

Whatever else we did to meet the needs of these girls, this was always the most important thing that we could offer them – unconditional love and support.

7

MEETING FURTHER NEEDS

Drug and alcohol addiction were at the bottom of most of the problems that our girls faced. If drugs were not the reason that they had become involved in prostitution in the first place, drugs had usually become part of the mix by the time they came to the Magdalene Group. We knew that in the end any other help we might be able to give these women would be short term and superficial unless they were willing and able to tackle their addictions. The key factor was always their willingness to admit their dependency and to break their habit. At the Magdalene Group we were willing to support the women all the way, from their first visit to the doctor or the drugs agency, through the course of their treatment and then afterwards as they built up a new drug-free life. But, in the end, the initiative and the will to go through with it had to be theirs.

We were blessed in Norwich with a variety of agencies that specialized in drug and alcohol dependency, though I am afraid that the demand for these facilities always outstripped the supply. The National Health Service provided various avenues into treatment, and there were other private and charitable agencies to which our clients could refer themselves. Some of these, like the

Matthew Project and Hebron House, were Christian organizations like us, but there were others that provided excellent services for both inpatients and outpatients. Hebron House was particularly useful to us because sometimes they were able to take mothers with small children into residential rehabilitation. Some of these agencies specialized in drug treatments, while others treated both drug and alcohol dependencies equally.

Each patient would be allocated a key-worker who would determine the best treatment, depending on the substance that was being misused, develop with the patient a personal care plan and keep in touch through regular interviews or visits. The rehabilitation centres could offer either residential or structured day programmes, as well as counselling and advice. The Magdalene Group always worked alongside such agencies as these and sometimes provided the woman's key-worker. We could offer our clients our drop-in centre every day as a point of contact, where they could also access courses and craft sessions that would occupy their time and their minds and, perhaps, open up new avenues of hope and interest. We did not offer a formal counselling service, since none of our staff or volunteers were trained counsellors, but we were able to offer ongoing friendship and support.

For some women detoxification only took a few days. The brave ones simply stopped taking their drugs and endured 'cold turkey'. Others embarked on a programme of reduction, aided by medical substitutes like methadone. The worst cases of both drug and alcohol addiction had to be under constant medical supervision as they withdrew or dried out, but others were able to detox at home. Either way, the crunch came when their detoxification was complete. The willpower and motivation needed to stay away from their old habits and their old companions was enormous, and girls needed every bit of support and encouragement that we and their friends at the Magdalene Group could give them. We sometimes linked a girl up with a mentor from her own peer group at the centre: another woman who had been through the same process and come out victorious on the other side. But the temptation to turn back and use drugs or take to the bottle again could continue for years, perhaps for the rest of their lives. We used to reckon that it would take as long for a woman to become established in her new lifestyle as she had been living with her addiction. The great advantage of the Magdalene Group was that we were there before, during and after the woman's treatment. We were able to offer a holistic approach that embraced the whole of a person's life and that of her family as well.

Addictions are nearly always a way of escape from inner pain. So many of our girls had suffered abuse as children, and the practice of prostitution is a kind of serial abuse, albeit in most cases a voluntary one. A loveless childhood, an experience of rejection, even a careless word of condemnation from a teacher or a friend, can cause an inner hurt which if reinforced becomes unbearable. Drugs and alcohol are painkillers. Therefore, the greatest help that we could give women trying to break a habit was acceptance and affirmation, a belief in their worth and that God had a better future for them if they would only take it. From somewhere or from someone they needed to acquire hope: the hope that life could be better for them in the future than it had been in the past. Sometimes the girls were motivated to kick their habits because they had become pregnant or given birth. The desire to keep the baby and to give the little one a mother's love and care was sometimes the stimulus they needed to do something that they would not otherwise have done for themselves. Others heard the wake-up call after they had been subjected to rape or extreme violence by a punter. They knew that the next time they might be the victims of murder. Such turning points in a woman's life would give us the opportunity to encourage them to take the first steps towards treatment and freedom.

One day one of our clients told us of a small family that she had allowed to live in her garage. The mother had two small children of 5 years and 9 months old. The mother was working on the streets in order to pay for drugs for herself and her husband. They had already fled from a violent situation in another part of the country and had ended up in Norwich, where they were homeless. It was winter, and when we saw the conditions in which they were living we knew that we had no option but to help them. They were afraid to approach the authorities in case they lost their children, but with our help they completed a housing application and agreed that we should involve the social services. I understood the difficulties of the local housing authority and the shortage of available accommodation, but after a temporary spell in a bedsit lent by another woman, they were offered a council house.

Tracey, the mother, had started to take amphetamines at the age of 23 and had soon moved on to heroin and out onto the streets to pay for her habit. We continued to provide a listening ear and any practical help we could at the Magdalene Group, but when Tracey received a three-week custodial prison sentence, her husband left her and her children were taken into care. Social services placed the children with Tracey's mother, and this turned out to be a long-term arrangement. It was the disintegration of her family that gave Tracey the incentive to sort out her life. She had reached the point at which she could see the rest of her life stretching ahead of her. If it was not to be a descent into irredeemable pain and misery, then she must turn round and take control of her habits.

When she came out of prison she embarked on a drug rehabilitation programme and managed to conquer her addiction. She moved in with her parents in order to be with her children and was doing well until one night she relapsed and injected herself again with heroin. This relapse nearly proved fatal. In the morning her mother found her unconscious and rushed her into hospital. There, the doctors had no alternative but to amputate one of Tracey's legs. She recovered, but now carries with her a permanent reminder of the terrible, destructive effects of drugs.

Since then Tracey has not reverted to her old habits; she has made a new life for herself. By her own choice, Tracey's children have continued to live with her mother, but she sees them every day and does her best to make up for the damage that drugs have caused in her life and that of her family. Tracey has also been brave enough to talk publicly about her past addictions and to participate in anti-drugs campaigns. She has spoken in front of various groups of people, including a national conference, where everyone was impressed by her courage as well as by her ability as a public speaker. Who can tell what might have been with so many of our women, if drugs had not taken hold of them and ruined their early lives?

◆ ◆ ◆

We discovered that most of the girls with whom we came into contact were in poor health. Quite apart from the adverse effect of drugs on their physical and mental health, working on the streets brought its own risks of infection and disease. Obviously they were especially vulnerable to the sexually transmitted diseases like gonorrhoea, syphilis and chlamydia, and their drug use would expose them to others, such as hepatitis B and C, but worst of all, they feared HIV/AIDS. Drugs also trigger many mental health problems, and we discovered that, compounding everything else, nearly 80 per cent of our clients were suffering from some degree of clinical depression, schizophrenia or bipolar disorder.

We were constantly encouraging our clients to use the Well Woman clinics at their local surgeries or at the hospital. Many women were reluctant to have these checks for fear of what they might discover, so we always offered to go with them and help them deal with whatever emerged. We also encouraged them to make use of programmes that screened for breast and cervical cancer. Their mental illnesses required specialist diagnosis and treatment and for which there were rarely easy cures. The roots of mental illness are still imperfectly understood, but many conditions are triggered or exacerbated by psychedelic drugs.

As the Magdalene Group became a recognized agency working in the field of prostitution, the local health service providers supplied us with free condoms to hand out to the women on the streets. We decided to do this in the interests of harm reduction. We were aware that it was not only our clients who were at risk from sexually transmitted diseases, but their punters as well. The men who were their clients would often offer more money for unprotected sex, but every encounter could spread infection, not only to the two people immediately involved, but also to other people with whom they might be sexually involved afterwards. This could include wives or girlfriends who were unaware that their partners had been consorting with prostitutes. Few people seem to be aware of the prevalence of sexually transmitted diseases in our promiscuous society. There is some public awareness of the danger posed by HIV/AIDS, but other STDs, like incurable genital herpes, are much more widespread. A specialist in one of the big London hospitals recently remarked on the radio that if everyone stuck to one sexual partner all their lives, he would be out of work. But sadly he had no worries about his own job security.

One of the saddest of our duties at the Magdalene Group was to sit by the bedside of someone who we had befriended and helped, whilst she died. Drugs, alcohol and disease, never mind murder, could all bring these women to an early grave. I was with Deena when she was told that she was HIV-positive. As we travelled home afterwards, she asked me what would happen to her when she died. She was afraid. I began to tell her about Jesus, and later we read the story in Luke chapter 7 of the woman who came to Jesus in the house of Simon the Pharisee. Deena was overwhelmed by the grace of God, whose Son had shown such tenderness and love towards a woman like her. She was ready to learn more of this Jesus and of the hope that he offered. She began to read the Bible and to understand that even she could be forgiven and washed clean by the blood of Jesus, and that death need not be the end. Before she died, both she and her partner had given their lives to Jesus, and Deena had received the forgiveness and peace that Jesus alone can give.

Whatever form of contraception the women might or might not use, their profession always made them vulnerable to pregnancy. One of the simple facts of life, of which our society seems to have lost sight, is that the natural outcome of sex is a baby. Sometimes a woman who became pregnant welcomed the thought of the baby and it was the stimulus that she needed to change her life. But often the baby was either unwanted or the woman knew that she would be unable to care for it. Today abortion is available on demand, and indeed the scale of abortion in the UK has reached holocaust proportions. So, many of our clients opted for abortion without a second thought. If they asked for our advice we would refer them to Pregnancy Crisis Norfolk (now Pregnancy Choices Norfolk), one of a number of Christian centres nationwide that offers free, unbiased advice about the options open to women facing an unexpected or unwanted pregnancy.

We knew that PCN would not push a woman into any particular choice, but inform her about her options and offer to support her, whatever choice she made. Some women would choose to go ahead with an abortion. This often seems the simplest way at the time, and there is often much pressure from family and friends, not to mention the medical profession, to make this choice. But some women suffer from feelings of guilt and grief afterwards, sometimes for many years afterwards. PCN would inform women of these possible psychological consequences and they also provided a recovery programme for women who needed support following a termination. Other women would choose to continue with the pregnancy, give birth, and voluntarily offer the child for adoption. There are so many infertile couples longing for a baby, that this option can be a blessing to others as well as offering the best future for the baby. Public policy and perception overemphasize the importance of the blood bond between mother and child, and underemphasize the importance of love and security in the child's upbringing, from whomever that love and stability may be derived. A permanent, settled home, with loving adoptive parents is far better for a child than being shunted backwards and forwards between inadequate or abusive natural parents and a succession of foster parents and children's homes.

In his book *The Purpose Driven Life* Rick Warren writes, 'The Bible says, "You saw me before I was born and scheduled each day of my life before I began to breathe" (Ps. 139:16). While there are illegitimate parents, there are no illegitimate children. Many children are unplanned by their parents, but they are not unplanned by God. God's purpose took into account human error, and even sin. God never does anything accidentally, and he never makes mistakes. He has a reason for everything he creates.'[4]

When one of our girls did have a baby, everyone at the Magdalene Group celebrated this new life with her and gave her a helping hand. We could provide nappies and baby clothes, potties, buggies, cots, and all the ongoing support that a mother with a newborn baby needed. We had a mothers and toddlers morning at the drop-in, which enabled young mums to make friends with others, whom they could then arrange to meet elsewhere to chat and compare notes about their children and their progress. This sort of informal network, offering mutual support and advice, is particularly important in our society today. In days gone by, such support and advice was provided by the extended family, especially by grandmothers, but today these older women who have experienced both the joys and the tribulations of bringing up young children are, sadly, often missing. Our older volunteers at the drop-in often functioned as surrogate grandmothers, both to the young mums and to their toddlers.

Whichever decision a woman made about her pregnancy we tried to give her the love she needed and to help her in practical ways. That was how we saw our calling from God: not to judge but to express his love in action. God came in the person of his Son, Jesus, to intervene in our troubled world and bring hope into our troubled lives. We saw our work in the Magdalene Group in the same light. Not everyone received Jesus and the hope that he offered, indeed some very forcefully rejected him. But he never rejected them, and even on the cross he prayed for their forgiveness. Not everyone wanted to receive the help that we offered either, and that was their choice. But we always kept an open door, and prayed for God to bless them.

◆   ◆   ◆

It was vital that if a woman was to leave her lifestyle on the streets, she should not only turn her back on the old, but turn to embrace something new. This might be a new husband or a new baby or a new home, but for many it also needed to be a new way of making a living. Few of our clients had done well at school, and a sense of failure compared with their contemporaries had often contributed to their low sense of self-worth. So a main feature of our work at the Magdalene Group became the provision of opportunities for education and training. We bought two second-hand computers and, using volunteers who could offer IT skills, we taught the women to be computer literate. The spell-check released them from the fear of making spelling mistakes, and the ease with which mistakes could be corrected inspired them to try their hand at all sorts of writing. This literacy was the gateway to accessing other more formal courses, either in-house with us or through the local colleges of further education.

We secured funding from the Learning Skills Council to hire teachers to come in to the Magdalene Group and to lead short courses that would provide a first step on the ladder towards business or professional qualifications. We found that some of the teachers were excellent, while others patronized our clients. They might have good qualifications, but they did not always have a good attitude, and we had to ask them to leave. Again, some of our girls were able to flourish in the classroom at college with other students, while others lacked the social skills and confidence to survive in such an environment. At the end of the day, some of our women were outstandingly successful. One of our very first contacts had been Rachel, a mum who was not on drugs and had no pimp, but who was out on the streets to earn money for her son's school trip to France. She told us later that her dream was to do a course at the Open University. With our support and encouragement she eventually succeeded and took a degree in interior design. She went on to get a well-paid job, which paid all the bills and paid for the school trips too.

Clare had a very different background. She was the third generation of women in her family who had been out on the streets. She had been introduced to prostitution at the age of 16. She was not on drugs, but she was being pimped by an older man who had befriended her and groomed her and put her to work alongside several other women who he ran. We met Clare on the street one evening and invited her to come to the Sitting Room during the day. She did our basic IT training course in my office. She broke away from her pimp and moved to another part of the country. She got a flat in the town where she settled and enrolled at the local college. The last time we heard from Clare she had obtained a good qualification and an interesting job and was wryly amused to report to us that she was now paying income tax. Welcome, Clare, to 'normal life'!

In addition to formal education, we provided opportunities for the girls to discover other skills. Jan and Andrea were two of our volunteers who excelled at teaching crafts and handiworks. They started several classes that took place in the afternoons, introducing the women to glass painting, stencilling, and painting on silks. Some of their work was sold on a stall at the King Street Festival and at the Bishop's Garden Party! One Christmas the women made Christmas decorations that were sold at the Christmas Fayre in a neighbouring market town, and so popular were their decorations that they received orders for more. The proceeds of these sales went into our contingency fund to help with the women's needs and emergencies, but there were also unseen proceeds that went into the women's bank of self-esteem.

Jan and Andrea also acquired a sewing machine and taught some of the girls to make soft furnishings, cushions and curtains to beautify their own homes. As well as teaching practical skills, this also introduced the women to the fact that they could create something of beauty for themselves. Janine had a natural talent to paint. One day, we were being visited by a civil servant from the government Home Office in Westminster in connection with a review of government policy in the field of prostitution. This official noticed one of Janine's paintings on the wall of my office. She was so impressed with it that she offered her a commission to design the cover for the *Home Office Review* when it was published. Janine was rather daunted by the privilege but she produced her design, and anyone who obtains a copy of the review can see her painting on the cover. Not only did this give an enormous boost to Janine's self-confidence but she was well paid for her work as well.

Janine had never worked on the streets; she had been employed by an escort agency. But she had given up the work at the agency because of the disruption that it involved in the life of her family. She was bringing up two children, and when we met her she was up to her ears in debt. She brought me her black bin-bag, and step by step we sorted out her finances. It took a long time to clear her debts but in the end she managed to do it. For those whose lives and finances have always been in reasonably good order, it is hard to imagine the relief of someone who has lived under a burden of unmanageable debt and who finally gets their head above water and owes no one anything. There is a recovery, not just of financial equilibrium, but of self-confidence and self-esteem that affects every aspect of their lives. With the confidence and the skills that Janine had acquired at the Magdalene Group, not least in designing for the Home Office, she went on to become the manageress of an up-market shop in the city.

As often as possible we linked a woman up with one of our staff who became her key-worker. The key-worker would try to meet regularly with the woman and talk about her life and her progress. Each woman was invited to set her own goals. We would ask her about her dreams: what did she want to do with her life? How did she want to change? We then tried to help her to identify manageable steps towards achieving her dream, and we looked for ways in which we could assist her or put her in touch with others who could. From time to time we engaged the services of an outside agency that taught personal development. As the women could see their own achievements in attaining their goals, so their confidence grew and they dared to dream even bigger dreams.

One of our support workers, Michelle, undertook a two-year research project that we called SOUL: Soft Outcomes Universal Learning. The SOUL Record consisted of a series of worksheets that a key-worker could use on a one-to-one basis with a client. They covered three main topics: attitude, personal and practical. They explored a wide range of issues including how they felt about themselves and about other people. Soft outcomes are the sort of things that are not easily measured or quantified. For example, a client turning up for an appointment on time when they have not managed to do so in the past is an achievement that is worth recording. A client getting up at 9 a.m. to face the day instead of at 3 p.m. is a step towards normal life. No one is going to award a certificate for these achievements, but for someone who has hit rock bottom, they are the first steps on the way up. To record them is to record a mini-victory and raises confidence to press on to achieve more. Of course it was often a case of two steps forward and one step back, or even of one step forward and two steps back, but we were committed to persevering with anyone who wanted to persevere.

◆　◆　◆

One of our greatest successes was Rosie. She was the woman whom we had found at the beginning, drunk and incapable in an alleyway, selling herself for four cans of lager. Low cost – high price. We met her again when she came to the drop-in. On this occasion also she was drunk and incoherent. She smelt disgusting. Toni was on duty: she brought Rosie in and put her in the shower. When she came out Toni fixed her up with clean clothes, whilst her old clothes went into a plastic bag ready for the washing machine. Slowly her story came out.

She had had two brothers: the older one was clever; the younger one had special educational needs. One way or another the brothers got all their parents' attention.

Rosie wanted to be the pretty little girl with flowing locks, but her mother made her cut her hair short to make it more manageable. Rosie was never sure what her parents wanted of her, or even of whether her parents wanted her at all. At the age of 6 her mother sent her to a neighbour's house with some sewing to deliver. The man of the house exposed himself to her and took her out into the garden where he masturbated in front of her. Rosie was deeply disturbed but, as is usually the case, was too frightened to tell her parents about it. She tried to avoid going to the house again, but her mother insisted on sending her, in spite of the fact that she knew that the man had a criminal record as a sex-offender.

At the age of 12 Rosie began smoking. She knew that her father was fond of her, but he was deaf and weak and there seemed to be no boundaries in the house. When Rosie was 14 her mother introduced her to the contraceptive pill. This confused Rosie even further: did her mother not care what she did or whom she did it with? Soon she was having sex with the boys at school, drinking, clubbing, taking drugs and truanting, and her parents did not seem to take any notice. At 17 she had a baby and was allocated a council house of her own. There, however, she became lonely and depressed. She married and had a second child, but only three years later she and her husband were divorced. Later she met another man who moved in with her and gave her a third child. But he was violent and sent her out onto the streets. Her life continued to spiral downwards, until she was sent to prison for involvement in an armed robbery. Her family took care of the children while she was in jail. On her release she refused to go back to live with the man who had violently abused her and she was offered another flat. She tried to look after her children again, but the task was too much for her and she found her solace in drink and drugs, and went back onto the streets to pay for them. By the time we first met her at the Magdalene Group she had lost all self-respect and was past caring about anything.

At home the oldest daughter was looking after the two younger children. But at the age of 18 this girl also became pregnant and threatened Rosie that unless she pulled herself together she would never see her grandchild. Rosie was injecting heroin at the time and she developed abscesses and became seriously ill. One day, her youngest child, a boy of 11, found her collapsed and unconscious. She was taken to hospital where she was in a coma in intensive care for two weeks. During this time she could hear what was going on around her but she could not respond. One day, her 11-year-old son came to visit her. He sat at the bedside and cried; he thought that his mother was going to die. It was at that moment that Rosie decided to live. This was the turning point for her. It was not a religious conversion for Rosie, but it was what the Bible calls repentance: a turning round, a decision to turn away from the old life and to begin a new one. She determined that she would never use drink or drugs again. Eventually she recovered, and when she came out of hospital, she began to make choices about her life for the first time. She did not go back to her old ways. She trained for a new career and began to take responsibility for her family. In the end she was saved because her love for her family was stronger than her addiction. We had prayed many prayers for Rosie over the years, and God had answered them, at least so far.

All through the years Toni and I kept in touch with Rosie, and the Magdalene Group encouraged and supported her as she climbed out of the pit into which she had fallen. Today, Rosie's son is 24 years old, she has three grandchildren who she sees, she has a new partner and she manages a high-class restaurant. She is smartly dressed, and her middle-class friends would never dream that the lady whom they know now had had such a painful and shameful past. There is a way out – for someone who can find the motivation to take it.

8

THE WIDER WORLD

When we first stepped out at night onto the streets of Norwich to meet the women working there in 1992, we knew of only two or three others places in the British Isles where people were doing the same thing. Now there are more than fifty Christian projects similar to the Magdalene Group in the UK alone, involving about a thousand employees and volunteers, and with a case load of more than six thousand clients.

As the credibility of the Magdalene Group grew within our own city, and as the visibility of the work spread beyond Norfolk, so we began to receive visitors from other places, anxious to learn from our experience and to catch our vision. Sometimes a group of visitors would come for a day or two, sometimes for a whole week, to shadow our workers, see our premises, and learn about our methods. These visits were a wonderful opportunity for us to share our experience and explain our activities and our values. I also found myself being asked to go and speak to other groups around the country who wanted to start up a similar outreach to women caught up in prostitution. We were always ready to make our written documentation, setting out our policies and procedures, available to others. We did not suppose that we had a blueprint that could simply be copied by everybody else, but we did have some experience, and when it came to compliance with all the rules and regulations, there was no point in everyone reinventing the wheel. People took away whatever was useful to them, and we blessed them in following the vision that God had given to them. We soon found that groups that had started up as a result of visiting us were in turn passing on their expertise to others. These were exciting times and our growing relationships with other projects were a great blessing to us all.

In 1995 a few of these groups working in the same field met together to pool ideas and information. All of them were Christian groups with the common aim of giving women working in prostitution the opportunity to change their lives if they wanted. Over the next few years it became clear that the work was spreading rapidly and that new groups were being established that needed help, advice and support. In 1998 a conference was held to offer training and encouragement to projects that had recently started or that were being developed. Out of this conference a national organization was launched in 1999 that was called the National Christian Alliance on Prostitution (NCAP). A development team was formed made up of managers and team leaders from existing projects, of which the Magdalene Group was one. In 2003, NCAP was incorporated as a registered charity in its own right to facilitate collaborative working and ensure continued growth along sound lines, of the work to which God had called us. I have been and continue to be a trustee of NCAP, and through my continued involvement with the national organization I have had the privilege of seeing a younger generation taking up the challenge and blazing new trails in the work.

NCAP's activities have developed to include training for both new and existing teams. We have produced various pieces of literature, including a series of leaflets which explore issues surrounding prostitution and sex trafficking, substance misuse and domestic violence. These are combined with a CD-ROM in a resource pack called *Breaking the Chains of Injustice – Responding to Sexual Exploitation in the UK*.[5] This pack is designed to inform people about the reality of life for women and men in the 'sex industry'. It is intended for use by churches, home groups, and secular organizations like the Women's Institute. The fact sheet alone would open the eyes of many people to the scale and nature of the problem:

- There are an estimated 85,000 individuals working in prostitution in the UK
- 75 per cent are female
- Two thirds get involved before their eighteenth birthday
- Children as young as 9 are abused through prostitution
- Individuals involved in prostitution encounter extreme levels of violence on a daily basis
- In the UK, the number of men purchasing sex has doubled in the last 10 years
- A pimp controlling a number of girls can earn up to £6,000 per week
- A 'compliant' female can earn a trafficker up to £120,000 per annum.

NCAP's biggest resource is a *Good Practice Guide* published in 2007, in which we have tried to bring together all the information and guidance that a project needs to set up and monitor its activities. The purpose of such a detailed guide is to make sure that groups working in this field are not sloppy or amateur, but are operating to the highest standards, in compliance with the law and with best practice in this area of social work. Only groups operating to these high standards are going to win and hold on to the confidence of the other agencies with which they need to work, if they are really to assist their clients in escaping their present bondage and finding freedom and a better future. There are so many ways in which work of this sort can go wrong that appropriate safeguards need to be built in from the beginning. The NCAP material is designed to forestall some of the mistakes that lie in wait for the well-meaning but unwary do-gooder. Anyone venturing into this field needs to be aware that they are dealing with extremely vulnerable adults and children, and that in the background there may be highly organized and dangerous criminal gangs.

Through its director and staff NCAP also provides a consultancy service, a point of reference to which groups can turn when they face a new problem or difficulty. The chances are that another project has encountered a similar difficulty before, and NCAP can serve as an exchange for information and advice. There are now regional networks of Christian groups involved in outreach to men and women engaged in prostitution, and the NCAP conference has become an annual event.

NCAP has recently changed its name for general purposes to Beyond the Streets. The new title gives a better description of the aims of the organization. A national resource and study centre has been established. Information about Beyond the Streets and its resources can be accessed through the website at www.beyond thestreets.org.uk or at www.ncapuk.org. Affiliation to NCAP is open to groups that are specifically Christian, although NCAP is willing to make its policy documents and procedures available to anyone who wants to use them. But we believe that as Christians we have distinctive values that we bring to this work. We believe in the value and dignity of every person as a human being created in the image of God. However defiled or spoiled that image may be, we believe in the possibility of redemption and change. We resist any attempt to pigeonhole our clients as 'prostitutes', preferring to refer to them as men and women engaged in prostitution. It is an important distinction: people do not gain their identity, for good or ill, from what they do, but from who they are in the sight of God. Furthermore, we believe that anyone can be enabled, if they want to be, to exit the lifestyle of prostitution. We believe in the possibility of transformation, not just of behaviour but of hearts and minds, through the love of God, often first made real in the love of our staff and volunteers on the streets. We do not believe that anyone is condemned, either by their personal history or by the 'sort of person they are', to a life of degradation and shame. As Christian groups we can also draw on the resources of local churches wherever we are: a resource that is still an incomparably rich store of goodwill and sacrificial commitment to the poor and needy.

NCAP and its affiliated groups have had an important voice in national consultations into various aspects of prostitution and trafficking. In 2003 the government Home Office initiated a review into the law regarding prostitution and the regulation of the sex industry – the first such review for more than fifty years. A Home Office official came to visit us at the Magdalene Group as part of the information gathering exercise that went into this review. As a result of this visit, I was invited to take part in many of the consultations and seminars that took place in London and to contribute from the insights that we had gained from working with women on the streets.

When the Home Office review document was published in 2004 under the title *Paying the Price*,[6] I was able to offer an overview and response from the Magdalene Group direct to the Home Office. NCAP was also in a position to make an informed response, on behalf of the Christian groups working in the field, to the ongoing consultation process that eventually produced a government document, *A Co-ordinated Prostitution Strategy*, in 2006.

Through such wider involvement, NCAP and its affiliate projects, including the Magdalene Group, were called upon for newspaper articles and television and radio interviews both locally and nationally, whenever the subject of prostitution came into the news. In 2006 the Magdalene Group was featured in the *Politics Show* on BBC television. A crew filmed the work of the project, coming out onto the streets with us at night and visiting the drop-in centre. We were careful not to exploit the women or intrude into their private lives, but we felt that it was important to show the world the realities of prostitution and to put out a warning to the younger generation. We were also pleased to be able to show off some of our achievements: what was happening at the Magdalene Group was, after all, good news. We were fortunate in having Charles Clarke as our MP. He was also, for a time, the Home Secretary. He visited the project in Norwich on a couple of occasions and we heard that he always spoke well of us in Parliament.

I could never have guessed when we first stepped out onto the streets in 1992 how much our work and our connections would have expanded in the following fifteen years. I never set out to be involved with government policy or to appear on television; I just followed the leading that I was given by God one step at a time. The expansion of our outreach into so many fields made for some hard decisions for me and for our trustees as to the best use of my time, but I felt that it was right to take up these opportunities that were being offered to us to have an input and an influence in the wider world.

◆ ◆ ◆

In January 2006 I was invited to attend the International Christian Conference on Prostitution to be held that April at Green Lake Conference Centre, Wisconsin, USA. This was the second such conference to be held in America, and it was to be the start of something even bigger for me and for this work worldwide. At the 2006 conference there were more than two hundred delegates, from thirty-seven countries and from all five continents. They all represented Christian projects that set out in one way or another to reach and help people trapped in a lifestyle of prostitution. It was at this conference that Bronwen Healy, who had authored a book called *Trophy of Grace* about her own experience as a drug addict and prostitute, encouraged me to write the book that you are now reading.

It was amazing to discover how God was raising up people all over the world to serve women in prostitution. There were people at the conference who were in the very early stages of starting a work: like the person with a vision for reaching women on the streets of Beijing, whose work was so sensitive that no names or address-es could be publicly given and a couple whose vision was to evangelize the estimated six hundred thousand women working as prostitutes in Iran. Some of the longer-established international Christian organizations like Teen Challenge and Youth With A Mission were also represented, with projects in several different cities from Mumbai to the Philippines. An outreach in Kolkata, India, was an outreach of the Assemblies of God Church in that city; other projects were more like the Magdalene Group, working in partnership with various churches in Norwich. Some groups, such as a ministry in Kigali, Rwanda, were specifically evangelistic, while others, such as an outreach in Istanbul, Turkey, focused on providing economic alternatives for women in prostitution. Most of the projects represented at ICCP concentrated on reaching women and girls, but some were directed towards men and boys, such as a man from India who had a particular ministry to male transvestites.

One of the testimonies was by a man from Nigeria, who had committed his life to taking the Gospel to those trapped in prostitution. He told a heartbreaking story, but one that must be only too common in Africa. He had come from a large family, but both of his parents had died. His oldest sister had gone to the big city and they didn't hear from her for two years. Then she contacted him. She said that she wanted him to study – he was apparently the brightest member of the family – and that she would pay for him to go to college. She paid for his studies for several years. While he was at the university he became a Christian. Shortly afterwards he discovered how it was that his sister was paying for his studies – through prostitution. He carried on at the university for another three months, but then his conscience would not let him continue any longer and he gave his studies up. Then he discovered that his sister had AIDS. She died, but she also had become a Christian before her death. This young man had then dedicated the rest of his life to helping women like his sister, forced by poverty into prostitution and then early death from AIDS.

One of the most impressive stories that I heard in Wisconsin was that of Annie Dieselberg. Annie had gone to Thailand as a missionary in 1994 but had felt drawn to

work with women in prostitution through Rahab
Ministries in Bangkok. This is her testimony.

Here is my journal entry for 22 June 2000:

I got a glimpse of hell tonight when we went to Super
Queen bar. When I got to the top floor, I looked in and saw
everyone was nude. I turned around to leave. The three of
us stood there in the doorway debating and then decided to
go in and pray. It was so dark. Not even a pretence of glamour. Just audacious evil. There was a wall full of idols and
shrines. A huge foot-long phallic symbol lay at the altar. A
girl came in and lit incense candles at the altar. The place
was so bad that I couldn't watch the girls on stage for long.
They were doing tricks I won't describe, using their bodies
to entertain through perversion. It was so degrading. Their
faces exposed their shame and misery. It was a prison of
hell. It was Satan's domain. I hated all of it – it's haunting.

It took quite a few visits before the images in these bars
would not haunt me through the night. Through the years
I have learned that there is evil in the world that is far
darker than anything I could have imagined. The influence
of evil can so consume a person that they will be willing to
rape and sell a woman into prostitution just for their own
financial gain. That same evil is not only willing but eager
to rape and photograph a child and sell the image around
the world just to add it to a collection. That same evil is able
to penetrate governments and bribe police to turn their
heads away at injustice and abuse for financial gain. That
same evil denies girls the opportunity for education and
leaves them ill-equipped to cope with a progressing society.
That same evil whispers in the girls' heads night after night,
'You are nothing, no one cares, this is all you will ever be,'
and convinces them that they have no other options. I have
learned that evil wounds its victims until they become

bound in a sinful lifestyle that they did not choose, and yet
for which they will be judged by the very people who
wounded them and by those who turned their heads away.
Women who end up in prostitution can only take so much
of this most intimate violence and assault before they begin
to lose a sense of themselves. One young woman I've
known through the years came to me one day after calling
in a desperately drunken state. I noticed scars all up and
down her wrists. I rubbed my fingers over her scars and my
eyes questioned her. She said to me, 'Sometimes I don't
know if I am still alive. I don't know if I am still a human
being. When I cut myself, I see blood and I feel pain and
then I know that I am still here.'

These women hide their real selves behind masks, but it
did not take me long to realize that prostitutes are simply
women who ended up in prostitution. I discovered them not
to be bad, sexually immoral, lustful, dangerous women, but
precious, gentle, caring and sensitive women. I discovered
mothers concerned for their children, daughters sacrificing
for their mothers. I began to see their hearts behind their
masks and hear their words through their tears, 'I never
thought I would do this.' 'I am not that kind of woman.' 'I
have to drink alcohol in order to do this.' 'I cried every night
for the first month.' 'I miss my kids.' 'I hate this job.'

Through working at Rahab I got to know the hearts of
women in prostitution and I am grateful to Patricia Green
and Lamduan Jinlee for allowing me to serve with them at
Rahab. Through that time I also became exposed to the sexual exploitation in the Nana area. I was shocked to find
large numbers of Cambodian and Vietnamese children
exploited as vendors, selling items throughout the night to
foreign men in the bars and often sexually exploited as well.
The situation weighed heavily on my heart.

I also became aware of Eastern European women in the
area. One young 18-year-old from Uzbekistan was brought

to us after she managed to escape her traffickers and we came to realize that large numbers of Russian-speaking women were trafficked into the Nana area. My colleagues and I began to envision a centre in the Nana area that would reach these women and children as well as the thousands of young Thai women exploited in the sex shows and bars.

I began to sense God's call to pursue the vision that had been growing inside me, but I was confused because I was committed in my work at Rahab. In October 2004, when I could finally deny God's call no longer I left Rahab but did not know what my next step would be and I entered a season of prayer. In January 2005 I joined with several other women who shared my vision and we began NightLight to bring light to women and children in sexual exploitation in the Nana/Sukhumvit area. Within a month we had two women who had left the bars and needed employment, and so our jewellery business began. Now, one year later, we have twenty women employed in the jewellery business. We have added two full-time Thai staff and many volunteers to supervise, mentor and administer the many tasks that need to be done. The outreach team is out on the streets twice a week visiting women and children from as many as eleven different countries. We offer them a job, but our goal is to see them come to life transformation through the power of God as they come to know Christ.

The vision that God has given us is huge and still unfolding step by step. When I stepped out of my comfort zone and walked in the devil's playground I quickly realized that I was out of my league. I began to experience how important it is to be totally dependent on God. It is not easy. Way too often I get in the way with my ideas and my impulsivity. Walking in the devil's playground requires dependency on God and his leading. I have discovered God in the shadows. I have discovered God as intimate, as powerful, as gentle, as miraculous, as passionate about justice, and as patient, not willing that anyone should perish. I have learned just how amazing God's love really is, and how passionately God wants us to show his love and grace to the hurting and the broken.[7]

I wonder whether the men from Europe and America who go to Thailand for stag parties or as so-called 'sex tourists', realize how much degradation and misery they cause these women in their search for their depraved pleasures.

The outcome of the 2006 International Christian Conference on Prostitution was the formation of a permanent body to co-ordinate the work throughout the world. It is now called the International Christian Alliance on Prostitution (ICAP). You can find out more about ICAP today by visiting their website at www.icap global.org, and you can find out more about NightLight, including purchasing their jewellery, at www.nightlight international.com.

Twenty years before the conference in Wisconsin I had had a strange dream. In it I had simply seen a globe. The dream had stayed with me over many years without me understanding what it could possibly mean. At ICCP I realized that God had prepared me to be part of something he was doing worldwide. Walking by the lake at that beautiful conference centre I was humbled and grateful.

◆ ◆ ◆

Back at home in the Magdalene Group we had also been branching out into a new area of work – in schools. Everyone knows that in every walk of life prevention is better than cure, and we hoped that by educating children in secondary schools about the dangers of prostitution we might be able to prevent another generation of young people being trapped in it. We ourselves had already seen third generation children being groomed for this way of life. We produced *The Jigsaw Project* which we could offer to schools in the city and the county. It was aimed at young people in school years 8 and 9, which means aged 12–13. We trained some of our own staff and volunteers to go into the schools to deliver the project that was designed to take about two hours of teaching time. We used a number of visual aids, including the video produced by Barnardo's that I described in Chapter 4 – *Whose Daughter Next?*

The aim of the *Jigsaw Project* was to raise awareness in young people of the dangers of harm and exploitation to which they might be exposed. We hoped that it might enable them to recognize relationships that might become abusive, and to know how to extract themselves from them before it was too late. More positively, we wanted to encourage these boys and girls to think about what constitutes a healthy relationship and what boundaries were appropriate in their sexual behaviour. We realized that these lessons might bring to light all sorts of abuse which these children were already subject to – for some it might be more than just a matter of raising awareness, it might be touching on some very sensitive areas. So we had put in place points of referral for pupils who might want to talk something through afterwards. We set up a *Jigsaw* telephone helpline, manned by members of the presentation team, which pupils could call, and we discussed fully beforehand with members of the school's pastoral staff the issues of confidentiality and child safety that might arise.

Although the Magdalene Group had a fairly narrow focus as far as relationships went, we wanted to open up the wider questions of what healthy sexual relationships are. Schools have taught sex education for many years and recently to increasingly young children but it has done little, if anything, to stem the rise of teenage pregnancies, sexually transmitted diseases and abortion amongst the young. It is not so much sex education as such that today's children need – they seem to be all too well informed about the facts of life and how babies are made from their earliest years at school. What many desperately need is 'love education'. So many adults today, let alone their children, think that love is spelt s-e-x, and that sex is spelt l-o-v-e. Neither is true. There are many forms of love that do not involve sex: the love of God, the love of parent and child, of brother and sister, the love of the poor. On the other hand, there are also many forms of sex that do not involve love. At the Magdalene Group we spent our lives dealing with the victims of loveless sex. One of our dear girls once said to me, 'What's it like to be in love, Theresa? I have never been in love, and I don't suppose I ever will be, doing the sort of things I do.' My heart bled for her. Another woman working in prostitution said, 'I just feel like a spittoon for semen.' Loveless sex is a bitter pill for all concerned. So we tried to alert the children, not only to the more extreme dangers of sexual exploitation, but also to the importance of putting sex into the context of a loving relationship. 'What is love?' we asked them, and tried to encourage them to fill out what they would want from a relationship with someone of the opposite sex.

There were opportunities for discussion, some of which took place in gender-specific groups. We encouraged the pupils to consider who they might talk to if they ever found themselves in a relationship or a situation that they could not handle. This enabled them to think about their relationship with their parents, their teachers, and for us to tell them of the various outside agencies that existed to which they might turn. Before we left we gave them a card with the number of our own helpline and told them that there was a member of the school staff who was available to follow up any issues that we might have raised in their lives. As with all our contacts at the Magdalene Group we tried to convey to the pupils that we were a non-judgemental organization, and that we only wished to see them making responsible decisions, free of coercion and in a way that was in their own best interests.

On the other side of the prevention work, we were happy to promote the efforts of CROP, the Coalition for the Removal Of Pimping. CROP is a voluntary organization working to end sexual exploitation and abuse of children and young people by pimps, traffickers and paedophiles. It was founded by a friend of mine, Irene Iveson – someone who had visited the Magdalene Group in the early days to learn about all aspects of our work. Irene's own daughter had been murdered, and Irene had written a book called *Fiona's Story* about her tragedy. CROP does excellent work through their parent support unit in alerting parents to the signs that their children, either boys or girls, might be the target of pimps or others who might exploit them sexually. Parents are warned to look out for such signs as these, especially if the signs are associated with a new, older boyfriend or girlfriend:

- Mood changes (more than the usual adolescent ones), confrontational attitudes, telling lies, staying in bed all day.
- Changes in appearance and dress.
- Different language, street talk and swearing.
- New possessions such as a new mobile phone that neither you nor she has purchased.

- Truanting from school.
- Missing from home, staying out overnight.
- Giving up old friends.
- Drug use.
- Using a new name.
- Excessive use of the computer and the Internet.

None of these signs would be an infallible indication that a child was being groomed for prostitution, but an alert parent might pick up a clue from these if something unhealthy was developing.

Whether from the parental end or from the pupil's end we hoped that our educational work would prevent at least some vulnerable young people from being trapped, as so many of our clients had been, in a life of prostitution.

◆   ◆   ◆

In 2005 I was amazed to learn that Kathy Browne, the Community Manager of Kettle Foods, one of our corporate funders at the Magdalene Group, wanted to nominate me for a Sieff Award, presented by Business in the Community in honour of Sir David Sieff of Marks & Spencer. These awards are made to individuals based in the community who have best collaborated with business to benefit society.

My amazement only increased when I heard that I had been shortlisted for an award, and that I should attend a Gala Dinner in Kings College, Cambridge. There, on a beautiful evening in June, I was presented with one of the East of England Regional Awards. As I sat at our table in that august hall I could not help reflecting how far God had brought that little girl from the East End of London, and how far we had come in the Magdalene

Group from those first cold nights on the streets of Norwich. Praise to him who had given me the courage to follow his calling.

9

PROSTITUTION AND THE LAW

The review that the British government began in 2003 with the consultation paper *Paying the Price*[8] was an example of a debate that has been taking place in many countries in recent years over the role of the law in relation to prostitution. Through the involvement of both the Magdalene Group and NCAP, I was impressed by both the thoroughness and the objectivity of the consultation process. I felt that there was a genuine desire on the part of the Home Office to find the best solutions to the many social problems surrounding prostitution. I believe also that the ministers and civil servants involved in the review gained a greater understanding and appreciation of the contribution that voluntary and faith-based organizations like ours were making in this field. In expressing her appreciation of our involvement in the consultation, one senior civil servant wrote to me, 'Your project members are simply amazing – I have been completely blown away by what they manage to achieve day in and day out in such challenging circumstances. It has been a privilege and inspiration to work with you.' Not the usual civil service jargon!

This review raised fundamental questions about the role of the law and what it can be expected to achieve, as

well as more detailed questions of strategy. As a
Christian, I believe in the rule of law. Paul wrote in
Romans 13:1, 'Everyone must submit himself to the governing authorities, for there is no authority except that
which God has established. The authorities that exist
have been established by God.' But there is a limit to
what the law can be expected to achieve. It cannot make
sinful men and women perfect. The most that it can do is
to restrain the worst excesses of sinful human nature.
Nevertheless, that is an important role in society and
needs the wisdom of Solomon to fulfil it. We can make
the mistake of expecting too much of the law, and politi-
cians are sometimes guilty of raising such unrealistic
expectations: 'Vote for us and all your problems will be
over.' On the other hand we can become cynical and give
up trying to reform or improve the law, as if, whatever
we did, it would not make any difference. It does.

The law sends messages to society. Paul calls the law
'a schoolmaster' (Galatians 3:24, KJV): it teaches us lessons about right and wrong. When abortion was illegal
it sent the message that killing unborn children was
wrong. That did not stop abortions from taking place in
the back streets. It did deter ordinary law-abiding people
from seeking abortions and persuaded them to look for
other ways of coping with unwanted pregnancies, for
instance adoption. It also deterred irresponsible, pre-
marital sex. The punishment for carrying out abortions
also deterred people from performing them. The legali-
sation of abortion, on the other hand, signalled that
abortion was a socially acceptable way of dealing with
an unplanned pregnancy; abortion lost its social stigma
and the abortion rate ballooned to monstrous proportions. In the same way the laws criminalizing murder
and theft do not prevent murders and thefts from taking
place. But they do deter people from murdering and

stealing from their neighbours, and they signal to us all that murder is not an acceptable way of settling quarrels, and theft is not an acceptable way of making a living. So most people do not kill and do not steal.

The function of the law in general is to preserve the peace within our society and to protect those who are least able to protect themselves. Paul tells Timothy that we are to pray for those who govern us 'that we may live peaceful and quiet lives' (1 Tim. 2:2). Solomon describes the function of the righteous king: 'He will judge your people in righteousness, your afflicted ones with justice . . . He will defend the afflicted among the people and save the children of the needy; he will crush the oppressor' (Ps. 72:2,4). Those are the functions for which God has established the powers that be: peace, justice and protection. But the New Testament also recognizes that the work of redemption, either of individuals or of societies, is something that the law cannot achieve. That is the work, not of the State, but of the Gospel and the Church.

But how are these principles to be applied to the issue of the law and prostitution? The answers we give will depend on the view that we take of prostitution. The English Collective of Prostitutes claims to represent prostitutes in England. It campaigns for the recognition of prostitution as a legitimate career choice and a legitimate business. It sees itself as a trade union for prostitutes. This organization is against any criminalization of paying for sex. The only role of the law, in their opinion, is to protect people who have chosen to work in prostitution from rape and violence, like anyone else. Everyone can agree with that objective at least. Beyond that, all I can say is that in many years of working with such women on the streets of Norwich I never met anyone who belonged to the English Collective of

Prostitutes and I never met anyone who did not want to leave the lifestyle if they could. The very name of this organization suggests a level of political, if not ideological, awareness that the women I met did not have, and far from campaigning for better pay and working conditions, our clients were too preoccupied with keeping their lives from falling apart altogether. Perhaps there are some upper-class prostitutes working as escorts for whom such representation is a priority, but we did not meet them out on the streets at night. As part of the Home Office consultation, the Magdalene Group was given a questionnaire that we asked our clients to fill in. One of the questions was, 'Do most women working in prostitution want to get out?' Every one of our women who responded to this questionnaire answered, 'Yes'.

So I was encouraged to read at the very outset that the government review took the same view of prostitution as we did. The then Home Secretary, David Blunkett, opened the discussion in *Paying the Price* by saying:

> Prostitution can have devastating consequences for the individuals involved and for the wider community. It involves the abuse of children and the serious exploitation of adults – many of whom are trafficked into and around the UK for this purpose. It has close links with problematic drug use and, increasingly, with trans-national and organized crime.[9]

This was the best starting place for a review of the law regarding prostitution: to begin by regarding all men and women working in prostitution as victims. Even if a few of them are not, the vast majority are. Many of them are the victims of others: of their abusers, their pimps or their traffickers. Some are the victims of their own wrong choices, in taking to drugs or becoming trapped in a cycle of poverty, homelessness and addiction. Those who do not start out as addicts, often become addicts later, as either their pimps seduce them into dependence or they begin drug or alcohol abuse to dull the pain and the shame of what they are doing. Once engaged in prostitution, too many become victims again, of abusive and violent clients who rape, assault and even murder them.

The government review therefore focused on three key issues:

- Prevention – through the education system, alerting children and parents to the dangers of exploitation and, through all the agencies involved in the care and protection of children, to identify young people at particular risk.
- Protection and support – providing help and advice for those already involved in prostitution and offering pathways out of it.
- Justice – bringing abusers, pimps and traffickers to justice, and providing justice and a safe environment for communities blighted by prostitution.

These were the lines along which we at the Magdalene Group were keen to see government policy develop.

When the *Co-ordinated Prostitution Strategy* was published in 2006, there was indeed a strong emphasis on the need for prevention. Our own work with the *Jigsaw* project in schools and the work of CROP had been featured in *Paying the Price*,[10] and such initiatives in schools were commended and encouraged. Everyone recognized that preventing young people from being drawn into the drug culture was a high priority, with much wider implications than just the link to prostitution. The importance of making all professionals working with children and young people – teachers, school nurses, accident and emergency staff at hospitals, doctors, sexual health clinics and teenage pregnancy services – aware of the warning signs that a young person might be at risk of being drawn into prostitution was also recognized. Some of the risk factors are: children missing education, children missing from home, children in or leaving the care system, children living in a prostitution environment, and children arriving unaccompanied in the country. Any of these factors might indicate a vulnerability to exploitation by unscrupulous adults, and should alert professionals to watchfulness and carefulness.

There was an equal emphasis in the *Strategy* on developing routes out. The government recognized that providing escape routes from prostitution requires a holistic approach, such as that which we had developed at the Magdalene Group. So intertwined are the problems of prostitution, addiction, debt, homelessness, mental and physical health, educational underachievement and lack of self-esteem, that no approach can be successful which does not try to integrate care and help across all these areas. The government also recognized the importance of outreach to those engaged in prostitution. Men and women involved in prostitution, with all the associated problems that tend to accompany it, are the least likely to seek help from official agencies such as social services or even GPs. The development of trust and confidence between a woman on the streets and a caring outreach worker is the key to accessing mainstream services.

These government documents were inexplicit about how and by whom these elements of the strategy of protection and support were to be provided. Many of the projects featured in these documents were voluntary ones and, like the Magdalene Group, faith based. There are features of the nature of this work that perhaps make it likely that voluntary bodies will be more effective in gaining the trust of women working in prostitution than statutory ones, and faith-based initiatives offer a level of commitment and motivation in staff and volunteers that statutory organizations cannot match. But this is part of a much wider debate about the relationship between voluntary and especially faith-based initiatives and the statutory services. It raises difficult questions that have not been resolved about the place of such initiatives in a secular society. Christian initiatives like the Magdalene Group tend to come under suspicion as being a cover for proselytism. The secular world finds it difficult to understand unconditional love of the sort that we tried to offer, and finds it even more difficult to believe that we could offer a gospel of salvation to those who wanted to hear it without making acceptance of it a condition of our help. Until these issues are clarified, State or local government support or funding for faith-based organizations will continue to be difficult.

In the end it seems a pity if the question cannot be settled by asking the simple question, 'Does it work?' Is society really interested in helping the disadvantaged and oppressed or is it more interested in political correctness? If the first, then why should society not endorse and support works that produce effective and successful outcomes, even if the work is carried out by Christians, and even if the outcome is that some of the client group become Christians themselves? It works, and what can be wrong with men or women engaged in prostitution finding a new life in Christ. As Stagecoach tycoon Brian Soutar once asked, 'What would you rather be doing: walking the streets having sex with strangers to pay for your drugs or being comforted by God?' Funding looms large in the lives of those involved with voluntary organizations but, in the long run, it may be better for them to depend on their own fundraising efforts than to be, or even to be thought to be, controlled by the government. But at least in the areas of prevention, protection and support, government agencies and voluntary organizations are agreed on the aims and objectives of the *Strategy*, and can plan to work together in some sort of partnership to improve the lives of those involved in prostitution.

When it comes to justice, the dilemmas are harder to resolve. Historically, most countries, including Britain, have criminalized the women and men who work as prostitutes. In Britain, paying for sex is not in itself a punishable offence, but loitering with intent, soliciting and advertising sexual services for payment is a crime, though a minor one. There is a fundamental contradiction, however, between treating people engaged in prostitution as criminals and treating them as victims. This was the contradiction that I faced when I was serving as a magistrate on the bench: I was treating the girls who came up before us as criminals, but I could see more and more clearly that they were victims, for whom punishment was not the answer. Across the world most of the recent reforms of the law regarding prostitution have moved in the direction of decriminalizing the people working in prostitution. This same movement has, paradoxically, taken place both where prostitution has come to be accepted as a legitimate lifestyle and also where those involved in it have come to be regarded primarily as victims. But the law has borne down on other groups of people in different ways.

Again, everyone agrees that the people most deserving of being criminalized are the pimps and traffickers – those who exploit men or women in prostitution for their own gain. It is no easy matter to track down and bring to justice those engaged in such activities but, nevertheless, the law should be clear and rigorous in punishing those responsible for so much human misery. In Britain, the Sexual Offences Act 2003 tightened the law against the sexual exploitation of both adults and children, clearly recognizing that, whatever might be thought about adults, children under 18 years of age are not capable of making a mature and informed decision about selling themselves for sex. This Act also strengthened the law against those involved in the exploitation of adults in prostitution, which includes the classic pimp as well as the trafficker, at home and abroad, and created a new offence of keeping a brothel. As a result of this Act, one Ann O'Brien was found guilty in 2005 of controlling prostitution in three south London brothels, and benefiting from this to the tune of more than two million pounds over a period of six years. This is not a trivial offence.

The men and women engaged in prostitution are not the only victims. The residents of a red-light district can suffer harassment and abuse as a result of the trade being carried on outside their front doors. Pedestrians and passers-by can find themselves pestered by kerb-crawlers, and the association of drugs and prostitution can bring other undesirable characters and activities into a neighbourhood where prostitutes are working. The detritus of used condoms and syringes can litter the streets and the gardens of such a neighbourhood, something that the residents obviously resent. In the light of these and other problems, various legal solutions have been proposed and tried in different countries over the last few years.

The Dutch have tried a model of providing 'managed areas' in their cities where prostitution is tolerated and supervised. The idea at the beginning was that within a managed area certain facilities would be provided for the women working there, an area would be designated for soliciting and maybe another for the brothels and other places where sexual services could be performed. In these areas, health and welfare provision could be made available to the men and women engaged in the trade. This approach basically accepted the argument of the Prostitutes' Collectives: that prostitution is a legitimate lifestyle choice and a legitimate business. The aim of this legislation was to remove from prostitution the elements of victimization: to remove the women from victimization by pimps, traffickers and drug dealers, and to provide them with areas where they could ply their trade in relative safety; and also to remove the trade from areas in which it victimized neighbouring residents or businesses.

Some of the problems with this approach would have been obvious from the beginning; others only became apparent as time went on. Where are the areas in our cities and towns where this trade can be licensed without causing nuisance and offence to other people? Something like this approach has been tried out informally by the police in some cities in Britain. But a journalist reporting on such an experiment in Scotland wrote, 'Zones were not created to help the women, but to dump them somewhere away from "respectable folk". The zone in Edinburgh was an insult to the women – a horrible, dangerous place with no proper protection.'[11] Big cities like Amsterdam or London may be able to identify 'red-light areas' where everyone in the neighbourhood is there either because they are engaged in the sex industry or at least tolerant of it, but in smaller towns and cities other people are always going to be offended if their residential or business district is turned into an area designated for prostitution.

In any case, the attempt to free the women involved in prostitution from victimization by putting them into 'managed areas' has been notably and predictably unsuccessful. It is not so easy to separate the women either from their pimps and traffickers or from their drugs. To supervise and control the trade, even in a closely defined managed area, requires such an intensive use of time and manpower by the police and local government agencies that it is difficult to maintain it long term. What started out as a vision of women freely choosing to engage in the profession and being offered a safe haven in which to pursue it, has largely foundered on the harsh realities of exploitation and addiction which, on the contrary, are their normal experience. Such an approach might work for women coming into the profession as adults for the first time, without a history of substance abuse or exploitation, if there are any, but it does not work for women or men who are already addicted or already controlled by others. The Dutch have found that, either the managed areas have to accept a level of drug abuse and exploitation amongst the women, or the women are forced out of the managed areas, back onto the unmanaged streets. Either way, this leaves the women victims just as before. As a result, while some managed areas continue to operate in the Netherlands, others have been forced to close. The British government rejected this solution.

In common with the Netherlands and Greece, some states in Australia have tried another approach: not of designating 'managed areas' but of simply licensing brothels. It was hoped that licensed brothels would allow the authorities to monitor and control the practice of prostitution, provide appropriate services to the women involved and verify that no under-age or trafficked girls were involved. In the event, none of these hopes has been fulfilled – indeed the opposite effect has been created. The existence of licensed brothels, far from decreasing the number of unlicensed brothels has actually led to their increase. The Attorney General of Victoria (Australia) reported that the brothel legislation had not prevented the growth of the illegal sex industry. In fact the number of unlicensed brothels in Melbourne had trebled in twelve months. Nor has rigorous control of the trade, even in the licensed brothels, proved possible either. Many of the brothels, the licensed as well as the unlicensed, remain in the hands of cartels and syndicates, with many of the women remaining in virtual slavery. Such legislation, far from restricting the abuses of the sex trade, has led to their increase.[12] In the Netherlands, the Van Traa Commission found that the organized crime associated with prostitution had increased rather than decreased following the licensing of brothels.[13] It appears that the licensing of brothels sends the message that the trade is socially acceptable, and so encourages its growth and proliferation. In any case, those women with problematic drug use are excluded from the licensed brothels and resort to the streets again, where all the old problems resurface untouched. Neither the designation of managed areas nor the licensing of brothels has actually helped the women involved to escape from their real problems of addiction and exploitation. The British government has rejected both.

There remains one new approach that has shown signs of making a real impact on the problem, that used in Sweden. Recent Swedish legislation decriminalized the sellers of sex, recognizing that they are more sinned against than sinning, and instead criminalized those who buy sex from them. In Sweden there are now no equivalents to the English offences of loitering or soliciting – the paying for sexual services, on or off the street is a criminal offence. This approach seeks to diminish the trade, not by tackling the supply side, but by tackling the demand for it. It seems to be successful. Since the new policy was introduced, the number of women involved in street prostitution has significantly decreased.[14] This policy of reducing demand can only work if there are real alternatives accessible to the women so made 'unemployed'. So this approach must be used in conjunction with the strategy of support and the provision of ways out such as programmes to support women leaving prostitution. It was this two-pronged attack on the problem that most recommended itself to the Home Office in Britain. The 2006 *Strategy* document included a whole new section on *Tackling Demand*.

In terms of street prostitution there was a new emphasis on the existing offence of kerb-crawling. An interesting initiative had been successfully trialled by the Hampshire police. Persons arrested for the first time for kerb-crawling had been offered an alternative to prosecution: participation, at their own expense, in a re-education programme designed to challenge their behaviour. The course explained the impact of street prostitution both on the women concerned and on the local community. The implications of a prosecution and conviction for kerb-crawling were also explained, in terms of the fines and punishments available to the courts, and also in terms of the shame and disgrace involved in public exposure in the local press. Of the 304 kerb-crawlers involved in the trial of this programme, only 4 were known to have re-offended, an unprecedented rate of success with any type of crime.

As a result of this whole process of consultation and strategy design, a clause was included in the Policing and Crime Bill 2009 to create a new offence in England and Wales of 'paying for sex where the provider is controlled for gain'. This seems to be a very precisely and accurately aimed legal arrow. It is what is called a 'strict liability offence', which means that the prosecution does not have to prove that the offender knew the man or woman was being controlled for gain, only that that was in fact the case. Since it is extremely difficult for a punter to know whether the woman he is paying for sex, whether on the streets, in a massage parlour or anywhere else, is in fact being controlled for gain, the law provides a very strong disincentive to engage in the practice at all. Objections to this change in the law have been raised on the basis that it interferes with a person's human rights: that if the trade involves a willing buyer and a willing seller it should not be criminalized. But these objections are baseless when viewed from either side, that of the seller or the buyer. If the seller is genuinely willing and not being 'controlled for gain' by someone else, there is no offence. On the other hand there is no human right for the buyer to be a party to the exploitation or enslavement of another person whatever he may pay or whoever she may be. The evidence that a high percentage of women involved in prostitution are the victims of others is overwhelming, and using the law to reinforce this message in the minds of those who access their services can only be good.

The new law in Sweden has resulted in the percentage of men purchasing sex from prostitutes decreasing from 13.6 per cent in 1996 to 8 per cent in 2008.[15] That should be compared to the statistics in Britain where the number of men purchasing sex has doubled in the same period.[16] The reduction in demand for sex as a commercial transaction must be the most effective way to tackle all the problems of exploitation: if the market is not there, fewer people will be drawn into the market-place to supply it. One of the principal reasons why the women are there in the first place, the entrapment of teenage girls by pimps and the trafficking of women by organized gangs, will be eliminated; there simply will not be the same money to be made out of them.

This new law will not in itself tackle the other reason why so many women enter prostitution: drug and alcohol addiction. There really is no legal remedy for this problem, although it is important to maintain the criminalization of dealing in drugs and of drunken and disorderly behaviour. These laws send important messages about the dangers and social unacceptability of such behaviour. But the root of the problem of addiction lies in social breakdown, especially the breakdown of family life and love, and in the consequent pain of rejection and despair. Neither of these problems is amenable to any quick fix by the British government or any other. There may be measures that governments can take to improve the situation, but it is at this point that we come up against the limitations of government action.

We come back here to one of the founding principles of the Magdalene Group and of other Christian organizations working in this field: that only Jesus can provide broken men and women with redemption from their fallen nature and from the hurts and injuries that have been inflicted on them in a fallen world. I have told the stories of some of the transformations of grace that we have been privileged to witness over the years in our work in Norwich. I know more surely now than when I first ventured out onto the streets in 1992 that, although many women can make progress with overcoming their problems and leaving the lifestyle of prostitution without a personal knowledge of God and the help of his Holy Spirit, the only full redemption from guilt and that gnawing sense of lack of self-worth lies in the knowledge of the love of God and of his Son, Jesus Christ. The law is good, but in the end it can only tinker with the problems of humanity. The real answers lie in Jesus, and in him alone.

10

AFTERWARDS

The road out of prostitution is hard and long, and there are no short cuts. As we have seen, most of the women caught up in this way of life have a history of abuse, often reaching back to childhood; most of them have long-standing addictions to drink or drugs; many of their lives are out of control and their self-respect, if it ever existed, is shot to pieces. Putting the pieces back together is a long and difficult process. Here is the testimony, not of one of our women working on the streets of Norwich, but of a New York call girl. Firstly, it explodes the myth of the glamour of executive-class prostitution. Secondly, it underlines the task that faces any woman coming out of a life of such abuse.

I was a New York call girl with my own book. My johns had careers in the fashion industry, finance, law and the media. I visited them in their homes, offices, and at well-known hotels like the Plaza. I also worked for madams in well-established brothels around the city. However, this is where any resemblance between my experience and the mythical 'call girl' ends.

I was a young teenage girl, not a sophisticated woman. I wasn't an independent agent, but controlled by a brutal pimp who had a stable of women. People believe only streetwalkers are addicts, but I abused drugs until well into my twenties. It was the only way I could cope with the physical, sexual, and emotional abuse that defined my job. As for my well-heeled clientele and their fancy suites, all I can say is, whether you turn tricks in a car by the Holland Tunnel or in the Plaza Hotel, you still have to take your clothes off, get on your knees or lie on your back and let this stranger use you in any way he pleases. Then you have to get up, get dressed and do it all again with the next one, and the next.

In the movies, call girls make lots of money which they invest in legitimate businesses when they retire from the life. It's taken me close to twenty years to undo the damage that was done to me in prostitution. Not only did I leave prostitution impoverished, I was totally isolated from mainstream society. The only people I'd had contact with for almost a decade were pimps, tricks and other prostitutes. I was deprived of a basic education; I had no job skills; my health was severely compromised. I required surgery and repeated medical treatment for reproductive damage and I remain infertile. In addition to these tangible issues, I've coped for years with the trauma resulting from years of emotional, physical and sexual abuse that is common in the lives of prostitutes. Like battered women who escape abusive partners, women escaping prostitution must totally rebuild their lives.[17]

Research suggests that it takes a woman at least six or seven years to accomplish the change; this New York call girl speaks of it taking her twenty years.

At the Magdalene Group we discovered that there are three stages in the transition: Stage 1 is when the woman decides to stop selling herself for sex and take her life in hand. Stage 2 consists of those steps that she needs to take to replace her old lifestyle with a new one. This includes all the aspects of rebuilding a life that we have traced in the work of the Magdalene Group: attention to housing needs, debt and financial management, freedom from addictions, health issues, education and training, and the growth of self-esteem that goes with succeeding in any of these areas. Stage 1 might be seen as the negative stage: simply stopping. Stage 2 is the positive stage of putting in place the elements of another, healthier, happier lifestyle. Helping and encouraging the women to negotiate these steps was the focus of the work of the Magdalene Group.

Some women might be engaged in this process for years. They were sometimes like people bungee-jumping. They would rise up, then plunge down again, in and out of the world of prostitution. We saw them make great strides in the direction of their new aspirations, and then something would happen that would set them back and they would go back to the streets or to their drugs or drink. It could be very frustrating for those of us who were trying to walk beside them; we needed endless patience. A woman might come to our Sitting Room regularly for months on end, take part in our courses, and work with us on the regeneration of her life. Then she would disappear off our radar altogether. We would lose sight of her and not know what had become of her. We would pray for her and commend her to God, who we knew cared about her even more than we did, but there was little else that we could do. Then, one day, she might reappear and start all over again. The outcome of a woman's engagement with the Magdalene Group was never a foregone conclusion but, nevertheless, there were many women who persevered or came back often enough to achieve their goal of a stable, new lifestyle: in which they were taking responsibility for themselves and for their family and children if they had any; in which a woman had a stable housing tenancy and was beginning to take a womanly pride in her home and her surroundings; in which she had control of her finances; and in which her life was no longer controlled by her cravings and addictions. It might be a lifestyle in which new opportunities for employment or education were opening up, and the possibility of new, more whole-some, relationships. She might be re-establishing con-tacts with family and friends that had languished or been broken off because of her prostitution. But even then, we discovered, there was another stage to the recovery of these women – Stage 3 – in which they still needed support and encouragement.

It is very difficult to re-enter normal society when you have a label from the past that brands you as either a prisoner, an addict or a prostitute – and many of our women were all three. Society can be very unforgiving, and it almost seems as if many people do not want to believe in the possibility of change. There is certainly a type of 'respectable' person, found in every social class, whose sense of their own worth depends on being able to look down on others and say, 'At least I am not as bad as them.' When one of 'them' does turn their life around, such people either do not or do not want to believe in it. 'A leopard can't change its spots,' they say. Sometimes, at least, the human leopard can: people *do* change. There *is* such a thing as redemption, but it is difficult for many people in society to accept or welcome it.

I began this book with two stories: the happier one was about Cara who did change, who did exit the lifestyle of prostitution, and with the help of God and Christian friends did find the new life of which she had dreamed. But along the way there had been several episodes in which she had fallen back into her old ways, and even many years later Cara still needed the love and support of people who knew her past and did not label or condemn her for it, people who loved her and wanted the best for her whatever she had done or whatever had been done to her. When Cara's little girl started at the local primary school, there were mothers at the school gate who found out about Cara's history. Sadly, both they and their children gave Cara and her daughter a hard time, turning their backs on Cara, while their little ones called Cara's 5-year-old daughter names that hurt and confused her. Cara herself was by then strong enough to deal with this verbal abuse: she realized that this was her neighbours' problem, not hers. But for her daughter's sake, she had to move the child to another school, out of the town, where she and her past were not known. Cara still needed support and reassurance.

It is no longer appropriate for girls like this to go to the Magdalene Group. The very association would perpetuate the label of 'prostitute' from which they are trying to escape. So in 2007 a group of these women contacted Toni, the pastoral worker, whom they had known at the Magdalene Group and asked if she could help them. By this time both Toni and I had retired from working with the Magdalene Group, and so we agreed to meet with them and discuss their needs.

We began by hosting a dinner party for this little group, to let them talk about their present lives and their needs. This dinner became a monthly event that has now been running for two years. We decided to work under the covering of a charitable Christian Trust that already existed, Community Action Norwich (CAN), whose premises we were offered for our use. We funded the dinner parties ourselves, but as the work developed we raised the funds to pay a part-time supervisor, Sarah. She has been joined by other trained and vetted volunteers, some of whom already have experience working with the Magdalene Group. They now meet regularly with some sixteen women who have come out of prostitution, eight of whom also have children. The programme is called STEP: Standing Together Encouraging People.

The list of STEP activities has now expanded to include not just the monthly dinners but other meetings and classes on a weekly basis. At the request of the women themselves there is a weekly Bible study that Sarah leads, followed by lunch together. Their souls are fed with the Word of God, their bodies with good healthy food, and they can ask for and receive prayer from one another. There is no compulsion or even expectation that women should come to this activity, but it is remarkably popular. Some of the girls have also followed a 13-week course called *Freedom in Christ* which enables them to deal with issues in their past and culminates with taking the 'Seven Steps to Freedom' at a day away. Many of the participants found the course extremely fruitful: they all felt that they had grown in their faith in God and had found the opportunities for questions and discussion particularly helpful. For some of them it was the first time that they had sustained participation in such a long course.

STEP also holds regular morning craft sessions where a variety of supporters come in to share their skills. These sessions are also followed by a lunch of soup, sandwiches, fruit and biscuits. We have 'pamper days' when volunteers come in to do the girls' nails and hair. We even have a professional hairdresser who takes the women to his salon and cuts and styles their hair for free. Nothing seems to boost the girls' self-image more than these days of pampering. It is not just that they feel more beautiful afterwards – perhaps more beautiful than ever before – but they realize that other people have spent their time on them and shown that they value them as people and as women. The diary for April 2009 announced the visit of 'a very friendly dentist' who was also willing to come and give his time free of charge to advise about dental hygiene. 'For all those who are terrified of dentists, come along and meet him in a really friendly environment, and ask all those questions you have always been afraid to ask.' Perhaps the most potentially fruitful of the offers of help that we have received is that from Janet, who works at the Job Centre in the city. Janet is a new Christian who now gives up some of her spare time to talk to the women about their employment needs and advise them of ways to access the job market.

As well as the meetings at which the girls can come together and share their mutual problems in an accepting and friendly environment, STEP also undertakes one-to-one pastoral work and home visits. One of the women, who had made a clean break from prostitution but continued to relapse into her drug habit, was found over Christmas to be self-harming. We accompanied her on hospital visits and follow-up appointments with her doctor. We managed to secure different medication for her to help her sleep, and the support and help that she received at this time enabled her to make the turnaround that she needed in her life. She made the decision to walk away from heroin for good and to distance herself from the drug culture and the friendships that she had made there. She started to redecorate her flat, after three years living in dirty and untidy conditions. She attended weekly sessions at an assertiveness and confidence programme, and began to look and feel better about herself. She also enjoyed and benefited from regular attendance at the STEP Bible study. It is still early days, but this woman has made great progress in these few months and she now offers support and encouragement to other girls struggling with similar issues.

One of the most satisfying aspects of the STEP programme as we watch it develop is the way in which the
women help and encourage one another. The meals that
we share together, as well as the appointments that they
make to meet at other times, are marvellous opportunities for them to chat to each other and share both their
triumphs and their failures. We find that they can challenge one another in a way that we could never do. It
would be easy for them to say to one of us, 'You don't
know what it's like,' and they would probably be right.
But when a sister from the streets tells them something,
it has the authority of personal experience behind it.

One of our best 'peer-mentors' is Annette. Annette was
the very first woman that we met on the streets in 1992.
At that time she was being pimped by a man who was an
alcoholic. It was her story that had so many echoes of my
own. In fact she'd had more material advantages as a
child than I'd had. She was born into a middle-class, professional family with a loving father who had instilled
into her good manners and good morals, but somehow
she had missed out on a mother's love. For a time she had
been a regular churchgoer. At the age of 12 she was over-
weight and was bullied at school. The family had moved
house on three or four occasions, so she had found it difficult to maintain friendships with people of her own age.
However, on leaving school she had qualified in secretarial work and had had steady jobs until she married. She
had loved her husband and he her, but he had been taken
ill and she had watched him die, leaving her a widow
with three children at the age of 33. I, too, had been widowed young, with two children, bereaved of a husband
that I had loved so much, so I had identified with her
from the first.

It was, however, seven years after that night when we
first met her on the streets that Annette came into the

Magdalene Group seeking help. Her story was that after the death of her husband she had lost her home and been forced to move into a council house, which she hated. She had subsequently met another man, Timbo. He was jovial and outgoing, everyone's friend. He seemed to love her and want to look after her and provide for her but it was all a deception: he turned out to be a confirmed alcoholic, and far worse was to come out about him in the ensuing years. Annette eventually discovered that he had a criminal record as a sex-offender of the worst kind, with a long history of abusing women and children. But by the time she found this out, it was far too late. After she had moved in with him, he became violent and manipulative towards her. As he had done with other women before, including his own daughter, he established control over her and then forced her to go out onto the streets and prostitute herself to pay for his drink and his gambling. She became terrified of this man and unable to resist his commands. Out on the streets, she had lost all her self-respect, and by the time that we met her again in 1999 she was living in a house that was filthy and full of smelly dogs, she was ill and her hair was falling out in tufts. In the midst of all this she still had two children living at home. She did not want to be doing what she was doing: she was a slave to Timbo.

It was a friend, Mary, also a woman on the streets, who finally persuaded Annette to come into the Sitting Room at the Magdalene Group with her. Mary had been helping Annette out by servicing some of Annette's clients for her. Timbo, at the time, had been stabbed in the leg and was recovering in hospital, which meant that Annette was unable to leave her children to go out onto the streets at night, but was also free to please herself in what she did during the day. In the evenings Mary was meeting some of Annette's regular clients and passing the money on to Annette to enable her to buy food. Such was the love and friendship that some of the girls showed towards one another. During the day Mary was able to bring Annette in to the Magdalene Group: perhaps, in the long run, an even greater service of love.

When I first talked to Annette, I asked her what her dream was. She said that she dreamed of escaping from her captor and living in a bungalow with two bedrooms and a little garden. I told her to start praying for it, and she still says that that day was the turning point in her life. People who have sunk so low often feel that God could not possibly want to know and will not listen to their prayers. But Annette found courage in my words, and started to ask God to help her. It took several years for the bungalow to materialize, though it did in the end, but sooner than that she found the strength and the courage to kick Timbo out for good. She knew by then that she had the support of her friends at the Magdalene Group and also of a friendly female police officer. From that moment on, Annette began to piece her life back together. She accessed all the help and the courses that we could offer and began to regain her self-respect. She picked up the threads of her childhood faith and started to pray regularly for God's help and provision. We talked to her about our own faith in Jesus: how we believed that God could forgive us our sins, however bad they were, and that Jesus had died for us all on the Cross. One day Toni and I had the joy of leading Annette in the sinner's prayer: she talked to God about her guilt and her shame, her weaknesses and failures, and she experienced that inexpressible sense of lightness and freedom that comes to all those who bring their sins to the foot of the Cross and receive the infinite mercy of a loving God. Annette committed herself to living the rest of her life for God's glory and asked for the help of his

Holy Spirit in making a new life for herself and her children. Toni went with her to the little church across the road from where she lived, and not long afterwards she was baptized, with all her new family from the Magdalene Group gathered around her.

Some time later she was invited to do some administrative work for her church and then for us at STEP. Secretarial skills had moved on from the shorthand and typing that she had done before her marriage, but she was an intelligent woman and she soon mastered the new technology and rediscovered the satisfaction of having a job and being part of a team. Her greatest contribution to STEP, however, has been, not her secretarial skills, but her ability to mentor other women like herself. She has proved to be one of the best at encouraging and supporting other STEP women as they in turn rebuild their lives, and follow in her footsteps.

It is fitting that Annette should both 'top' and 'tail' this book. Her story illustrates so much of what the Magdalene Group and now STEP have set out to do. The women we have met on the streets have all been people who, for one reason or another, have lost control of their lives and been forced into a way of life that they neither planned nor wished for. We have offered them help to regain control and to recover their self-respect. When we have been unable to help them ourselves we have introduced them to other people who could and, if they were willing, we have introduced them to Jesus who alone can fulfil all their needs.

STEP is still a very young initiative. With more funding and more staff and volunteers we could expand our activities in other directions. We have had offers, for example, of caravans in which the women and their children could have a holiday at the seaside. In any case, I expect the number of women accessing our services to grow. STEP is not an alternative to the Magdalene Group but an important follow-up to the outreach and mentoring that Magdalene offers. It is an important component of what happens to the women afterwards.

But even STEP is not enough. Some time before my retirement from the Magdalene Group I had seen the need for some residential accommodation for women exiting a life of prostitution and addiction. I dreamed of a house in which our girls could live in the security of a real Christian home – a place where they could realize their personal aspirations and where self-esteem and self-worth could grow naturally. Underpinning it all would be the support of loving Christian staff, people who could help them with their problems and assist them in planning for their future; staff who, without moralizing or condemning, would enable the love of God to be felt in the house.

People coming out of prison, prostitution and addiction all face similar problems in reintegrating into mainstream society. The statistics are staggering. Each year in the UK 180,000 people enter a programme of medical detoxification through one of the many drug treatment agencies, yet less than 4 per cent remain drug free afterwards. These statistics include our women off the streets who suffer from addictions.[18] With prisons the figures are equally appalling: 85 per cent of those in prison have offended before and 65 per cent of those in prison will re-offend within two years of their release – 30 per cent within 48 hours.[19] What abysmal failure and waste! What is needed is more care and accommodation afterwards.

The Nehemiah Project in South London demonstrates what can be done. This is another charitable trust with Christian motivation and inspiration. Nehemiah operates a course called *A New Direction* in two London prisons. The course lasts six months. Only about twenty prisoners can access it at any one time and it is always oversubscribed. During the course the men address their chemical dependencies and their criminal mindset, develop new life-skills, from reading and writing to skills applicable to the workplace. The parallels with the work of the Magdalene Group amongst people imprisoned in a life of prostitution are obvious. On release, the prisoners are encouraged to move on to a residential project in South London where their treatment programmes continue, and finally they move on again to another house where they continue to receive the support of staff and of each other, in preparation for full integration into mainstream society. It sounds a long, arduous and costly programme, and it is. But the results speak for themselves: after seven years 94 per cent of the graduates of the programme have not re-offended and 72 per cent of ex-addicts are still clean. Prison itself costs the taxpayer £37,000 per prisoner per year.[20] Anything else is cheap by comparison.

The Nehemiah Project demonstrates the importance and effectiveness of residential aftercare and support for prisoners and addicts, and our women exiting prostitution usually have exactly the same sort of background and needs. During my time as Director of the Magdalene Project I did not have the chance to explore the possibility of such a residential home for the girls any further. I had dreamed the dream, but was not able to make it a reality. I still have a great yearning to see such a house established that meets the needs of women in this region escaping from a life of prostitution, but maybe to start such a project is the calling of someone of the next generation. We each have to do the work that God calls us to do, and to do it as well as we can. But he accomplishes his purposes, not through any one individual, but through the whole body of Christ. I cannot do everything and

God does not depend on me to do it all. I depend on him, but he does not depend on me: he has others who will pick up the threads of the great tapestry that he is weaving and make it yet more glorious.

◆   ◆   ◆

So this story does not really end. My story will end one day when I go to be with the Lord, but the story of the women of the streets will never end. Prostitution is called 'the world's oldest profession', and it is not going to disappear any time soon. A woman who had been caught in adultery was brought to Jesus one day to see what he would say about her and her sin (John 8:2–11). Jesus refused to condemn her, but told her to go and sin no more. But perhaps his most telling words were to the men who had brought her, amongst them the most religious and 'righteous' people of his day. To them Jesus said, 'If any one of you is without sin, let him be the first to throw a stone at her.' And, one by one, they all went away. No one, man or woman, is without sin, in thought or word or deed, in this area of our lives. None of us can afford to throw stones at one another, and the universality of sexual sin means that there will always be those who become trapped in a life of degradation and despair, like the women whom I first began to see from the magistrates' bench, and then began to meet on the streets of Norwich.

But that does not mean that we can do nothing to help and save them. I was astounded to discover that in 1845 there was already an organization working in Norwich to minister to and rescue 'fallen women'. In those days it was described as 'affording asylum to females who having deviated from the paths of virtue, may be desirous of being restored to their station in society by religious instruction and the formation of moral and industrious habits.' That institution had ceased to exist somewhere in the intervening years but, in spite of the quaint language, I could recognize the same calling as that which I had experienced myself – a calling that had driven me and my fellow workers to go out onto the streets looking for these women in order to help those who had the will to change.

As I and those of my generation lay down the baton, I pray that God will raise up others, as he is doing abundantly, in Britain and throughout the world, to take it up and to bring the love of God to these women, whose hurts break my heart and his. If, through reading this book, you have been touched by God to be part of this work, then contact your nearest project through NCAP or ICAP, or if there is not one near you – then perhaps you could start one as I did! As we have seen, the Magdalene Group eventually employed several paid staff, but the work has always depended as much on a host of faithful volunteers: people who went out on the streets at night with flasks and biscuits, people who manned the drop-in centre, made tea and sandwiches and cooked meals, people who taught IT and other employment skills, who shared their joy in making beautiful things with their hands, people who gave us money and clothes and toys and food parcels and baked cakes, and people who prayed for us and for the women, both the women we knew and the men and women still out there in the dark whom we did not yet know. You too could be one of those people who work and pray and give their time and their love to the lost and hurting and broken. Perhaps with a few more people like that, another Gemma Adams need not end up face down in the Belstead Brook.

◆ ◆ ◆

I want to end this book with a poem that I came across some years ago. It takes me back to those days in my childhood when I waited in our front room in the East End of London to hear the strains of the Salvation Army band strike up at the end of our street. It tells of William Booth, the founder of the Salvation Army, and of his passion for the lost, amongst them the prostitutes of Victorian London on whose behalf he waged a long and eventually successful campaign. The poem also tells of that same passion that took me out onto the streets of Norwich and into the lives of the women of our own generation that have been similarly blighted. Although now retired from the Magdalene Group, I still have the same passion to help these women, who have become so precious to me. So, this is my testimony too.

I'LL FIGHT

A Review of William Booth's Last Public Message by Irena Arnold *(italics mine)*

In breathless silence they waited all
The people who crowded the great domed hall;
Our Founder oft had been there before
They had heard his messages o'er and o'er.
But somehow, he looked more frail that night,
As he came into view in the brilliant light:
His strength was ebbing, his eyes were dim,
But strong and brave was the heart in him.

The soldier's spirit, the prophet's fire,
Burst forth in his lifelong heart's desire;
A fiery passion for souls was there
Which seemed to electrify the air;
And, baring his heart to all the world,

He stood with the Blood and Fire unfurled;
And sent this challenge to foe and friend:
'I'll fight, I'll fight, to the very end!

'While children suffer, and cry for bread
I'll fight 'til they're warmed and clothed and fed.
While stricken women in sorrow weep,
While lost girls wander in anguish deep,
While men in a prison dark are bound,
While there is a drunkard to be found,
While one dark soul is without the light,
To the very end, I'll fight, I'll fight!'

His voice re-echoes through years gone past,
This stirring message that was his last.
We flash our answer in quick reply,
We'll raise the banner he held so high;
We'll fight on the field where our founder fell
For the Lord JEHOVAH he served so well,
And say as our life's full strength we spend:
'I'll fight, I'll fight to the very end.'[21]

ENDNOTES

1 Cited in *Signpost Series 3b* (NCAP, 2006).
2 Cited in *Paying the Price* (Home Office, 2004), Crown Copyright.
3 Herzog Jewell, Dawn, *Escaping the Devil's Bedroom* (Monarch, 2008). Used by permission.
4 Warren, Rick, *Purpose Driven Life* (Zondervan, 2002). Used by permission.
5 *Breaking the Chains of Injustice – Responding to Sexual Exploitation in the UK* (National Christian Alliance on Prostitution, 2007).
6 *Paying the Price* (Home Office, 2004), Crown Copyright.
7 The story of NightLight Bangkok is used by kind permission of Annie Dieselberg.
8 *Paying the Price* (Home Office, 2004), Crown Copyright.
9 *Paying the Price* (Home Office, 2004), Crown Copyright. Used by permission.
10 *Paying the Price* (Home Office, 2004), Crown Copyright.
11 Jean Rafferty, cited in Bindel, Julie, *Streets Apart* (Prostitution Research and Education, 2004).
12 Cited in *Paying the Price* (Home Office, 2004), Crown Copyright.
13 Cited in *Paying the Price* (Home Office, 2004), Crown Copyright.

[14] Cited in *A Co-ordinated Prostitution Strategy – and a summary of responses to Paying the Price*, p.35 (Home Office, 2006).

[15] Cited by the Nordic Institute for Gender Studies and Nordic Council of Ministers, 2008.

[16] Cited in *Prostitution in UK Factsheet* (National Christian Alliance on Prostitution, 2007).

[17] *Female Juvenile Prostitution: Problem and Response* (National Center for Missing & Exploited Children, 2002).

[18] *Channel 4 Dispatches: Mum Loves Drugs Not Me*, 03.11.08.

[19] *Guardian*, 04.03.08.

[20] www.nehemiahproject.org.uk

[21] Arnold, Irena, 'I'll Fight' first published in *Poems of a Salvationist* (Revell, a division of Baker Publishing Group, 1923). Used by permission.

ORGANIZATIONS QUOTED

Barnardos
www.barnardos.com

The Besom
www.besom.com

Beyond the Streets (see also NCAP)
www.beyondthestreets.org.uk

Coalition for the Removal of Pimping (CROP)
www.cropuk.org.uk

Full Gospel Business Men's Fellowship International
www.fgbmfi.org

International Christian Alliance on Prostitution
www.icapglobal.org

The Magdalene Group Norwich
www.magdalenegroup.org

National Christian Alliance on Prostitution (NCAP)
www.ncapuk.org

National Women's Refuge is now part of Women's Aid
www.womensaid.org.uk

Nehemiah Project in London
www.nehemiahproject.org.uk

NightLight Bangkok
www.nightlightinternational.com

Pregnancy Choices Norwich is part of a national
network at www.careconfidential.com

A Note From Theresa

If you wish to contact me with questions and comments, or if you just want to say 'Hi,' I can be reached by e-mail at

lchpbook@yahoo.co.uk

or

stepoffice1@yahoo.co.uk

or via my website

www.theresacumbers.co.uk

Also by Martin Down

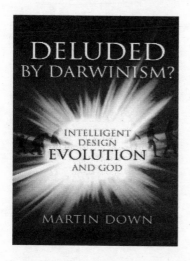

Deluded by Darwinism?

Intelligent Design, Evolution and God

Martin Down

For many years Martin Down believed what Teacher said in school . . . that the world evolved over millions of years, and all the species we see today were formed by random mutation and natural selection. But as a Christian he found a different account in the Bible.

Here was a conflict of ideas between scientists who, like Darwin, believed that the world was self-explanatory, and the Bible that said the world was created by God. But now, into the heart of the conflict, has come a new and astounding perspective: scientific evidence of Intelligent Design.

Could science itself now be leading to the reappearance of God? Martin Down invites us to reconsider the evidence.

978-1-84291-365-9

Also from Authentic

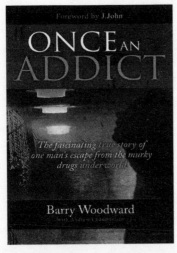

Once an Addict

Barry Woodward

Barry Woodward was a drug dealer and heroin addict who once lived on the notorious Bull Rings in the centre of Manchester. This book describes Barry's descent into the murky underworld of drug dealing, addiction, crime and imprisonment, and gives first-hand insight in to the city's nightlife and music scene, which was part of his world. Along the way we are introduced to some of the most extraordinary characters, and we see the extreme lengths to which some of them will go to get their next 'fix'.

Illegal drug use claimed the lives of many such people, and it seemed inevitable that Barry would also succumb to the drastic consequences of his addiction. With devastating amphetamine-induced mental health issues, a fourteen-year heroin addiction, a string of broken relationships, and the threat of HIV looming, the outlook for Barry appeared very bleak. Then three extraordinary encounters changed his life forever . . .

Barry Woodward is a national motivational speaker and the founder and director of Proclaim Trust. He and his wife Tina, live in Greater Manchester, England.

978-1-86024-602-9

Rebecca Andrews

Policing
Innocence

Is your child
really safe?

Policing
Innocence
Is your child really safe?

Policing Innocence

Is your child really safe?

Rebecca Andrews

Day after day the media reveals the latest cases of child abuse, but do we believe these could happen in our street, our church, our home?

Drawing on her professional expertise as a policewoman, as well as emotional investment as a mother, Rebecca Andrews navigates us through this challenging, yet critical issue, engaging us with a writing style full of humour and refreshing honesty.

In *Policing Innocence* we learn how child sex offenders operate within society, of the shocking frequency of paedophilia in churches, and we are introduced to a whole range of issues, from the Internet crisis to the law courts, from female abusers to the most common question Rebecca is asked: 'How do you do your job?'

Policing Innocence is not about scare-mongering, but rather is an attempt to expose the webs paedophiles weave to ensnare and destroy.

Rebecca Andrews has been an English police officer for many years. She has served on frontline duties as well as serving in the Child Protection Unit and Paedophile Unit. She is married with two daughters and involved in her local church.

978-1-86024-626-5